EDITOR: Maryanne Blacker

FOOD EDITOR: Pamela Clark

■ ■ ■

ASSISTANT FOOD EDITORS:
Jan Castorina, Karen Green

ASSOCIATE FOOD EDITOR: Enid Morrison

CHIEF HOME ECONOMIST: Louise Patniotis

HOME ECONOMISTS: Tracey Kern, Quinton Kohler,
Jill Lange, Alexandra McCowan, Kathy McGarry,
Kathy Snowball, Dimitra Stais

EDITORIAL COORDINATOR: Elizabeth Hooper

KITCHEN ASSISTANT: Amy Wong

■ ■ ■

STYLISTS: Marie-Helene Clauzon,
Rosemary de Santis, Michelle Gorry, Jacqui Hing,
Anna Phillips

PHOTOGRAPHERS: Bruce Allan, Kevin Brown,
Robert Clark, Andre Martin, Robert Taylor, Jon Waddy

■ ■ ■

HOME LIBRARY STAFF:

ASSISTANT EDITOR: Beverley Hudec

ART DIRECTOR: Paula Wooller

DESIGNER: Robbylee Phelan

EDITORIAL COORDINATOR: Fiona Nicholas

■ ■ ■

PUBLISHER: Richard Walsh

DEPUTY PUBLISHER: Nick Chan

■ ■ ■

Produced by The Australian Women's Weekly Home Library.
Typeset by ACP Color Graphics Pty Ltd.
Published by ACP Publishing Pty Ltd, 54 Park Street, Sydney.

■ ■ ■

♦ **U.S.A.:** Distributed for Whitecap Books Ltd by Graphic
Arts Center Publishing, 3019 N.W. Yeon, Portland, OR,
97210. Tel: 503-226-2402. Fax: 530-223-1410.

■ ■ ■

♦ **CANADA:** Distributed in Canada by
Whitecap Books Ltd, 1086 West 3rd St, North Vancouver
B.C. V7P 3J6 Tel: 604-980-9852. Fax: 604-980-8097.

■ ■ ■

Finger Food
Includes index.
ISBN 1 86396 008 2.

■ ■ ■

© A C P Publishing Pty Ltd 1993
ACN 053 273 546
This publication is copyright. No part of it may be reproduced
or transmitted in any form without the written permission
of the publishers.

■ ■ ■

FINGER FOOD

Here are around 200 tempting recipes, hot and cold, for the best party food ever! Some are easy some more elaborate, so you can mix and match to suit everything from a cocktail party through to a family barbeque. On the next page you'll find helpful party planning tips, then each recipe has do ahead, storage and freezing hints to help you even more. By "prepared", we mean up to the stage before cooking or completing. By "made", we mean ready to serve or assemble.

Pamela Clark

FOOD EDITOR

Hot Savories

Our instructions for doing ahead will save you time and stress. You'll know how to plan your party if you know what to do in advance. Some recipes can be prepared beforehand, others can be completed and reheated. To reheat savories, place in single layer on baking sheets, cover loosely with foil, slash holes in the foil about 2 inches apart, then heat in 350°F oven, unless otherwise specified.

PARTY PLANNING

A party at home is more fun if you are well organized. Planning is the key. Devise a selection of finger food that suits your guests' tastes and your budget, then make lots of lists.

Foodwise, make two shopping lists (one with items to buy ahead; the other with last-minute "perishables"), then plan your cooking timetable, starting with recipes that are suitable to freeze.
Take stock of "accessories", too. Have you enough serving plates and china, cutlery, tables, chairs, glasses, linen and so on? You may need trays if you plan to pass the finger food around.
Friends and relatives can often help with china, cutlery and glasses, but it may be more convenient to hire the things you need. Shop around before hiring; we found the variations in prices quite amazing.
To make things run more smoothly, consider hiring someone to serve and clean up. Many agencies provide these services and they are surprisingly inexpensive.

QUANTITIES: One of the most difficult decisions is how much food and drink you will need to supply. We have stated how many savories are made from each recipe. As a general guide, allow 6 pieces per person for the first hour, and about another 4 pieces for each further hour. We like a variety of hot and cold savories, depending on the season and the occasion. It's a good idea to take into consideration a mix of colors, tastes and textures. Young people tend to eat more, so serve extra crisps, crackers, nuts, pretzels, cheese and olives, etc.
To indicate the party is over, serve some lovely chocolates or petits fours with coffee where the occasion is suitable.

DRINKS: Drinks are even more difficult to estimate than food. You may wish to serve spirits or cocktails when guests arrive, or simply serve beer, wine (including sparkling and champagne style) and/or juice, mineral water and non-alcoholic drinks. Wine can be served throughout the party. It's helpful to put drinks in an accessible spot with someone to serve them.
Of course, don't forget the ice and plenty of napkins!

DUCK AND SPINACH MINI PIZZAS

1 package (¼oz) active dry yeast
½ teaspoon sugar
½ cup lukewarm water
1½ cups all-purpose flour
3 tablespoons vegetable oil
¼ cup tomato paste
1 tablespoon vegetable oil, extra
1 clove garlic, minced
2 boneless, skinless duck breast halves, sliced
½ bunch (10oz) spinach, shredded
¾ cup grated fresh Parmesan cheese

Combine yeast and sugar in bowl, stir in water, stand in warm place about 10 minutes or until foamy.

Sift flour into bowl, stir in oil and yeast mixture, mix to a firm dough. Turn dough onto lightly floured surface, knead for about 10 minutes or until dough is smooth and elastic. Place dough in lightly oiled bowl; cover, stand in warm place 30 minutes or until dough doubles in size.

Turn dough onto lightly floured surface, knead until smooth. Divide dough into quarters, divide each quarter into 10 pieces. Knead each piece into a smooth ball, press to flatten. Place rounds on lightly greased baking sheets, spread lightly with tomato paste.

Heat extra oil in pan, add garlic and duck, cook, stirring, about 2 minutes or until just browned; remove from pan. Add spinach to pan, cook, stirring, about 1 minute or until soft. Spoon spinach onto pizzas, top with duck, sprinkle with cheese. Bake 400°F oven about 10 minutes or until cheese is melted and pizza base cooked through.

Makes 40.

■ Pizzas can be made a day ahead, reheat in oven.
■ Storage: Covered, in refrigerator.
■ Freeze: Not suitable.
■ Microwave: Not suitable.

RIGHT: Duck and Spinach Mini Pizzas.

CURRIED VEGETABLE SAMOSAS

2 tablespoons vegetable oil
1 onion, chopped
1 clove garlic, minced
2 teaspoons curry powder
1 large (7oz) potato, finely chopped
1 small carrot, finely chopped
3 tablespoons frozen green peas
5 sheets (10in x 10in) ready rolled shortcrust pastry
1 tablespoon milk
oil for deep-frying

Heat oil in pan, add onion, garlic and curry powder, cook, stirring, until onion is soft. Stir in potato and carrot, cook 5 minutes or until tender, stir in peas; cool.

Cut 3 inch rounds from pastry. Top each round with 1 level teaspoon of potato mixture, brush edges with milk, fold in half, press edges together.

Just before serving, deep-fry samosas in hot oil until well browned.

Makes about 45.

■ Can be prepared 2 days ahead.
■ Storage: Covered, in refrigerator.
■ Freeze: Uncooked samosas suitable.
■ Microwave: Not suitable.

GLAZED CHICKEN BITES

1lb ground chicken
1 egg, lightly beaten
½ teaspoon ground coriander
½ teaspoon five-spice powder
2 teaspoons chopped fresh chives
½ cup fresh bread crumbs
GLAZE
½ cup redcurrant jelly
½ cup mango chutney
2 teaspoons lemon juice

Combine chicken, egg, spices, chives and bread crumbs in bowl. Shape rounded tablespoons of mixture into balls, place on baking paper-lined baking sheet. Bake in 400°F oven about 15 minutes or until well browned; drain on absorbent paper.

Just before serving, add chicken bites to glaze in pan, simmer for about 3 minutes or until lightly glazed.

Glaze: Combine jelly, chutney and juice in pan, stir glaze mixture over medium heat until combined.

Makes about 40.

■ Bites can be prepared 2 days ahead.
■ Storage: Covered, in refrigerator.
■ Freeze: Suitable.
■ Microwave: Not suitable.

BACON MINI POTATOES

14½oz can baby new potatoes, drained
1 teaspoon French mustard
3 thick slices bacon

Cut potatoes in halves, spread cut surfaces with a little mustard, trim a small piece from each rounded side to make level. Cut bacon into ¾ inch x 1¾ inch strips, cover flat side of potatoes with bacon, secure with toothpicks.

Just before serving, broil until bacon is crisp and browned.

Makes about 20.

■ Can be prepared 2 days ahead.
■ Storage: Covered, in refrigerator.
■ Freeze: Not suitable.
■ Microwave: Suitable.

BELOW: From left: Curried Vegetable Samosas, Glazed Chicken Bites, Bacon Mini Potatoes.
RIGHT: From left: Mini Steamed Pork Buns, Pepper Camembert and Bacon Wontons.

MINI STEAMED PORK BUNS

2 packages (½oz) active dry yeast
1 cup warm water
½ cup superfine sugar
2 cups all-purpose flour
1 cup self-rising flour
1oz lard, melted
FILLING
1 tablespoon vegetable oil
3 green onions, chopped
1 teaspoon grated fresh gingerroot
2 teaspoons cornstarch
¼ cup water
1 tablespoon light soy sauce
2 teaspoons hoisin sauce
1 teaspoon sugar
1 tablespoon dry sherry
½lb Chinese barbequed
pork, chopped

Combine yeast, ⅓ cup of the water and 2 teaspoons of the sugar in small bowl. Sprinkle with 2 teaspoons of the all-purpose flour; cover, stand in warm place about 10 minutes or until frothy.

Combine remaining sugar and sifted flours in large bowl, stir in remaining water, lard and yeast mixture, mix to a soft dough. Turn dough onto floured surface, knead for 10 minutes or until dough is smooth and elastic. Place in lightly oiled bowl; cover, stand in warm place about 1 hour or until dough is doubled in size.

Knead dough until smooth, divide into 48 pieces. Knead each piece into a ball, flatten each ball, place 1 level teaspoon of filling on center of each ball. Gather edges to enclose filling, pinch together to seal, place pinched-side-down on 1¼ inch squares of baking paper. Place buns about 1¼ inches apart in steamer; cover, cook over boiling water about 10 minutes or until buns are dry to touch. Remove paper before serving.

Filling: Heat oil in pan, add onions and gingerroot, stir over heat 1 minute. Stir in blended cornstarch and water, then sauces, sugar, sherry and pork. Stir over heat until mixture boils and thickens, remove from heat; cool.

Makes 48.

■ Buns can be made a day ahead, reheat in steamer for 4 minutes.
■ Storage: Covered, in refrigerator.
■ Freeze: Cooked buns suitable.
■ Microwave: Not suitable.

PEPPER CAMEMBERT AND BACON WONTONS

½lb slices bacon, finely chopped
¼lb pepper camembert cheese,
finely chopped
24 egg pastry sheets
1 egg white, lightly beaten
oil for deep-frying

Cook bacon in pan, stirring, until crisp; drain on absorbent paper. Place level teaspoons each of bacon and cheese on center of each pastry sheet, brush edges lightly with egg white. Fold sheets in half diagonally, press edges to seal. Brush 2 opposite points lightly with egg white, pinch together.

Just before serving, deep-fry wontons in hot oil until puffed and well browned; drain on absorbent paper. Serve hot.

Makes about 24.

■ Wontons can be prepared a day ahead.
■ Storage: Covered, in refrigerator.
■ Freeze: Uncooked wontons suitable.
■ Microwave: Not suitable.

GRUYERE AND PECAN PASTRY PARCELS

¼lb gruyere cheese, chopped
3½oz ricotta cheese
1 stalk celery, finely chopped
½ teaspoon chopped fresh rosemary
1 egg, lightly beaten
pinch cayenne pepper
3 tablespoons chopped pecans
6 sheets phyllo pastry
¼ cup (½ stick) butter, melted

Combine cheeses, celery, rosemary, egg, pepper and nuts in bowl; mix well.

Brush 3 sheets of pastry with some of the butter; layer together. Cut sheets into 3 inch squares, top each square with a level teaspoon of cheese mixture, bring corners together in center, press edges together firmly. Repeat with remaining pastry, butter and filling. Place parcels on lightly greased baking sheets, brush lightly with butter; cover, refrigerate 1 hour.

Just before serving, bake in 375°F oven about 15 minutes or until browned and crisp.

Makes about 36.

- Parcels can be prepared a day ahead.
- Storage: Covered, in refrigerator.
- Freeze: Uncooked parcels suitable.
- Microwave: Not suitable.

OLIVE AND SUN-DRIED TOMATO TARTLETS

½ cup whole-wheat flour
½ cup all-purpose flour
½ teaspoon paprika
2 tablespoons (¼ stick) butter
¼ cup grated fresh Parmesan cheese
2 tablespoons water, approximately
2 tablespoons grated fresh Parmesan cheese, extra

OLIVE AND TOMATO FILLING
1 tablespoon olive oil
1 onion, chopped
1 clove garlic, minced
1 small zucchini, chopped
⅓ cup chopped sun-dried tomatoes
⅓ cup pitted chopped black olives
3 tablespoons chopped fresh basil

Sift dry ingredients into bowl, rub in butter, stir in cheese and enough water to make ingredients cling together. Knead on lightly floured surface until dough is smooth; cover, refrigerate 30 minutes.

Roll dough between sheets of baking paper until ¹⁄₁₆ inch thick. Cut 2 inch rounds from dough, place rounds in 1¾ inch fluted tart pans, prick pastry all over with fork. Bake in 350°F oven about 15 minutes or until lightly browned; cool.

Just before serving, spoon mixture into pastry cases, sprinkle with extra cheese, bake in 350°F oven about 5 minutes or until heated through.

Olive and Tomato Filling: Heat oil in pan, add onion, garlic and zucchini, cook, stirring, for about 3 minutes or until onion is soft; remove from heat. Stir in tomatoes, olives and basil.

Makes about 40.

- Pastry cases can be cooked and filling prepared 2 days ahead.
- Storage: Pastry cases in airtight container. Filling, covered, in refrigerator.
- Freeze: Pastry cases suitable.
- Microwave: Filling suitable.

LEFT: Gruyere and Pecan Pastry Parcels.
BELOW: Olive and Sun-Dried Tomato Tartlets.

CHICKEN DRUMMETTES IN CRISP SPICY BATTER

12 (about 2lb) chicken wings
3 tablespoons besan flour
¼ cup self-rising flour
½ teaspoon chili powder
½ teaspoon garam masala
¼ teaspoon ground cumin
¼ teaspoon ground coriander
½ cup water
oil for deep-frying
SAUCE
½ cup Chinese barbeque sauce
¼ cup water
½ teaspoon chopped fresh chilies

Cut first and second joints from wings. Holding small end of third joint; trim around bone with sharp knife. Cut, scrape and push meat down to large end. Pull skin and meat down over ends of bones; they will resemble baby drumsticks.

Sift dry ingredients into bowl, gradually stir in water.

Just before serving, dip drummettes into batter, deep-fry in hot oil until lightly browned and cooked through. Serve hot with sauce.

Sauce: Combine sauce, water and chilies in pan, bring to boil.

Makes 12.

■ Wings can be trimmed 2 days ahead. Batter can be prepared 3 hours ahead.
■ Storage: Covered, in refrigerator.
■ Freeze: Uncooked wings suitable.
■ Microwave: Sauce suitable.

SMOKED FISH AND HERB VOL-AU-VENTS

3½oz smoked cod, skinned, boned
2 egg yolks
1 tablespoon mayonnaise
2 tablespoons chopped fresh chives
1 tablespoon chopped fresh parsley
½ teaspoon French mustard
¼ cup grated cheddar cheese
1 egg white
2 x 2oz packages oyster cases

Blend or process cod, egg yolks and mayonnaise until smooth. Transfer mixture to bowl, stir in herbs, mustard and cheese; mix well.

Just before serving, beat egg white in bowl until soft peaks form, fold into fish mixture. Spoon mixture into oyster cases, place on baking sheets. Bake vol-au-vents in 350°F oven about 10 minutes or until lightly browned.

Makes 24.

■ Filling can be made 3 hours ahead.
■ Storage: Covered, in refrigerator.
■ Freeze: Not suitable.
■ Microwave: Not suitable.

LEFT: Clockwise from left: Chicken Drummettes in Crisp Spicy Batter, Peppery Cheese Puffs, Smoked Fish and Herb Vol-au-Vents.

PEPPERY CHEESE PUFFS

1 cup water
3oz (¾ stick) butter
1 cup all-purpose flour
1 teaspoon seasoned pepper
3 eggs, lightly beaten
¾ cup grated cheddar cheese
¼ cup grated fresh Parmesan cheese
oil for deep-frying

Combine water and butter in pan, bring to boil, stirring, until butter is melted. Add flour and pepper all at once. Stir vigorously over medium heat until mixture leaves the side of pan and forms a smooth ball. Place mixture in small bowl of electric mixer (or in processor). Add eggs gradually, beating on low speed after each addition. Fold in cheeses; mix well.

Just before serving, deep-fry rounded teaspoons of mixture in hot oil until lightly browned and cooked through. Drain on absorbent paper.

Makes about 60.

■ Mixture can be prepared 3 hours ahead.
■ Storage: At room temperature.
■ Freeze: Not suitable.
■ Microwave: Not suitable.

9

MINI ROTI WITH SPICY TOMATO SAUCE

1 cup all-purpose flour
2 green onions, chopped
¾ cup boiling water, approximately
SPICY TOMATO SAUCE
2 teaspoons butter
2 cloves garlic, minced
¼ teaspoon grated fresh gingerroot
1 teaspoon ground coriander
½ teaspoon ground cumin
pinch chili powder
½ teaspoon turmeric
½ x 10oz can Tomato Supreme
¼ cup water

Sift flour into bowl, stir in onions, quickly stir in enough boiling water to mix to a soft dough. Turn onto floured surface, knead until smooth.

Roll 2 level teaspoons of dough into a thin sausage about 6 inches long. Repeat with remaining dough. Coil sausages, flatten between hands.

Roll flattened coils on floured surface into rounds about 3 inches in diameter. Cook rounds in lightly greased heavy-based pan, pressing flat with large spoon while cooking, until lightly browned on both sides. Serve roti hot with hot sauce.

Spicy Tomato Sauce: Heat butter in pan, add garlic and spices, cook for 2 minutes over medium heat. Stir in Tomato Supreme and water, bring to boil, simmer, uncovered, for about 8 minutes or until sauce is thickened.

Makes about 30.

- Roti can be prepared several hours ahead; reheat in oven. Sauce can be made 2 days ahead.
- Storage: Roti, covered, at room temperature. Sauce, covered, in refrigerator.
- Freeze: Not suitable.
- Microwave: Sauce suitable.

APRICOT CHICKEN TRIANGLES

1 tablespoon vegetable oil
1 small onion, finely chopped
1lb ground chicken
⅓ cup finely chopped dried apricots
½ teaspoon ground cumin
pinch chili powder
1 loaf sliced white bread
1 egg, lightly beaten
oil for deep-frying

Heat oil in pan, add onion, cook, stirring, until onion is soft. Stir in chicken, apricots, cumin and chili; cook, stirring, for 5 minutes; cool.

Remove crusts from bread, roll each slice with rolling pin until thin. Cut slices in halves diagonally. Lightly brush triangles with egg, top each triangle with ¼ level teaspoon of filling. Fold triangles in halves, press edges together with a fork.

Just before serving, deep-fry triangles until browned; drain on absorbent paper.

Makes about 40.

- Triangles can be prepared for cooking 2 hours ahead.
- Storage: Covered, in refrigerator.
- Freeze: Uncooked triangles suitable.
- Microwave: Not suitable.

BELOW: Mini Roti with Spicy Tomato Sauce.
RIGHT: From left: Apricot Chicken Triangles, Corn Puffs with Lemon Chili Sauce.

CORN PUFFS WITH LEMON CHILI SAUCE

1 cup cornmeal
1 green onion, finely chopped
½ cup fresh bread crumbs
½ cup self-rising flour
¼ teaspoon double-acting
    baking powder
1 teaspoon sugar
1 egg, lightly beaten
3 tablespoons taco sauce
½ small red bell pepper, finely chopped
¾ cup water, approximately
oil for deep-frying

LEMON CHILI SAUCE
2 tablespoons lemon spread
2 tablespoons taco sauce
⅓ cup water

Combine cornmeal, onion, bread crumbs and sifted dry ingredients in bowl, gradually stir in egg, sauce, pepper and enough water to make a stiff mixture.

Just before serving, deep-fry rounded tablespoons of mixture in hot oil until lightly browned and cooked through; drain on absorbent paper. Serve puffs hot with warm sauce.

Lemon Chili Sauce: Combine all ingredients in pan, bring to boil.

Makes about 25.
■ Mixture can be prepared 3 hours ahead. Sauce can be made 2 days ahead.
■ Storage: At room temperature. Sauce in refrigerator.
■ Freeze: Not suitable.
■ Microwave: Sauce suitable.

PARMESAN BASIL FRANKFURTERS

3 frankfurters
all-purpose flour
2 eggs, lightly beaten
1¼ cups (3½oz) grated fresh
   Parmesan cheese
3 tablespoons chopped fresh parsley
3 tablespoons chopped fresh basil
2 teaspoons ground black pepper
oil for deep-frying
TOMATO BASIL SAUCE
1 tablespoon olive oil
1 onion, finely chopped
2 cloves garlic, minced
14½oz can tomatoes
1 cup water
2 teaspoons sweet sherry
2 tablespoons chopped fresh basil
1 tablespoon chopped fresh parsley

Cut frankfurters diagonally into ½ inch slices. Toss slices in flour, shake away excess flour, dip into eggs, then into combined cheese, parsley, basil and pepper. Press cheese mixture firmly onto frankfurter slices; cover, refrigerate 15 minutes.
Just before serving, deep-fry frankfurter slices in hot oil until lightly browned; drain on absorbent paper. Serve hot with sauce.
Tomato Basil Sauce: Heat oil in pan, add onion and garlic, cook, stirring, until onion is soft. Stir in undrained crushed tomatoes, water and sherry, bring to boil, simmer, uncovered, about 20 minutes or until thickened; stir in herbs.

Makes about 40.

■ Frankfurters can be prepared
  2 days ahead.
■ Storage: Covered, in refrigerator.
■ Freeze: Suitable.
■ Microwave: Sauce suitable.

MINI CURRIED EGG PUFFS

3 sheets (10in x 10in) ready rolled
   puff pastry
4 hard-boiled eggs
2 teaspoons curry powder
2 tablespoons mayonnaise
1 tablespoon chopped fresh chives
1 egg, lightly beaten
1 teaspoon poppy seeds

Cut 3 inch rounds from pastry. Mash hard-boiled eggs, curry powder, mayonnaise and chives with a fork in bowl. Place 2 level teaspoons of mixture together in center of each pastry round. Lightly brush edges of rounds with beaten egg, fold rounds in half, press edges together.
   Place puffs on lightly greased baking sheets, brush lightly with egg, sprinkle lightly with poppy seeds.
Just before serving, bake puffs in 375˚F oven 12 minutes or until browned.
Makes 27.

■ Puffs can be prepared a day ahead.
■ Storage: Covered, in refrigerator.
■ Freeze: Not suitable.
■ Microwave: Not suitable.

SPICED APPLE MEATBALLS

1lb ground beef
1 small onion, finely chopped
½ cup finely chopped dried apple
1 green onion, finely chopped
3 tablespoons chopped fresh parsley
1 tablespoon brandy
¼ teaspoon ground cinnamon
pinch ground nutmeg
3 tablespoons chopped
   pistachio nuts
1 egg
1 cup (3½oz) fresh bread crumbs
2 tablespoons vegetable oil

Combine beef, onion, apple, green onion, parsley, brandy, cinnamon, nutmeg, nuts and egg in bowl; mix well. Roll 2 level teaspoons of mixture into a ball then coat in bread crumbs. Repeat with remaining mixture and bread crumbs. Heat oil in pan, add meatballs, cook until browned all over and cooked through. Serve hot.

Makes about 50.

■ Meatballs can be made 2 days ahead.
■ Storage: Covered, in refrigerator.
■ Freeze: Suitable.
■ Microwave: Not suitable.

LEFT: From left: Parmesan Basil Frankfurters, Spiced Apple Meatballs, Mini Curried Egg Puffs.

CREAMY SCRAMBLED EGGS IN FLAKY PASTRY CASES

2 x 2oz packages oyster cases
5 eggs
3 tablespoons butter
1oz cooked ham, finely chopped
2 tablespoons chopped fresh parsley
1 tablespoon heavy cream

Place oyster cases on baking sheet. Lightly beat eggs in bowl until combined. Heat butter in pan, add eggs, stir gently over heat until beginning to set; remove from heat. Stir in ham, parsley and cream. Spoon mixture into oyster cases, keep warm in 300˚F oven.

Makes 24.

■ Cases can be made 20 minutes ahead.
■ Storage: Not suitable.
■ Freeze: Not suitable.
■ Microwave: Not suitable.

ABOVE: From back: Creamy Scrambled Eggs in Flaky Pastry Cases, Seafood Bites with Lemon Ginger Sauce.
RIGHT: Seafood Rolls with Lemon Sauce.

SEAFOOD BITES
WITH LEMON GINGER SAUCE

½lb uncooked shrimp, shelled
½lb sea scallops
½lb boneless white fish fillets
1 egg
½ teaspoon grated lemon zest
2 tablespoons lemon juice
¼ cup chopped fresh parsley
oil for deep-frying

SAUCE
1 tablespoon cornstarch
¼ cup lemon juice
¾ cup water
1 small chicken bouillon cube, crumbled
1 tablespoon honey
1 tablespoon light brown sugar
1 teaspoon grated fresh gingerroot

Blend or process seafood, egg, zest, juice and parsley until well combined.

Just before serving, deep-fry rounded teaspoons of mixture in hot oil until well browned; drain on absorbent paper. Serve warm bites with warm sauce.

Sauce: Blend cornstarch with juice in pan, stir in remaining ingredients, stir over heat until sauce boils and thickens.

Makes about 50.

■ Fish mixture can be made a day ahead.
■ Storage: Covered, in refrigerator.
■ Freeze: Not suitable.
■ Microwave: Not suitable.

SEAFOOD ROLLS
WITH LEMON SAUCE

2 egg whites, lightly beaten
5 x 1¼oz seafood sticks, finely chopped
5½oz can crab, drained
1 teaspoon lemon pepper
4 green onions, chopped
15 sheets (6½in diameter) Thai rice paper

LEMON SAUCE
1 cup water
½ small chicken bouillon cube, crumbled
½ teaspoon grated lemon zest
½ cup lemon juice
pinch chili powder
2 teaspoons cornstarch
1 tablespoon water, extra
1 teaspoon chopped fresh chives

Combine egg whites, seafood, pepper and onions in bowl.

Soak rice paper sheets in water for about 1 minute or until soft; drain. Cut sheets in halves, place onto clean cloth. Top each half with 2 level teaspoons of seafood mixture, fold in long sides, then roll up from narrow ends.

Just before serving, place rolls in steamer in single layer, cook, covered, over simmering water until heated through. Serve hot with hot sauce.

Lemon Sauce: Combine water, bouillon cube, zest, juice and chili in pan, stir over heat until mixture boils. Stir in blended cornstarch and extra water, stir until mixture boils and thickens. Stir in chives just before serving.

Makes 30.

■ Rolls can be prepared 3 hours ahead.
■ Storage: Covered, in refrigerator.
■ Freeze: Not suitable.
■ Microwave: Not suitable.

Place oysters in ovenproof dish. Heat butter in pan, add onions and garlic, cook, stirring, until onions are soft, stir in herbs. Spoon over oysters, sprinkle with cheese. **Just before serving,** bake oysters in 350°F oven about 5 minutes or until heated through.

Makes 24.

■ Oysters can be prepared a day ahead.
■ Storage: Covered, in refrigerator.
■ Freeze: Not suitable.
■ Microwave: Suitable.

LEMON GINGER SHRIMP

30 (about 2lb) uncooked jumbo shrimp
2 teaspoons lemon juice
2 teaspoons grated fresh gingerroot
1 tablespoon light soy sauce
1 teaspoon Oriental sesame oil
pinch five-spice powder
2 tablespoons vegetable oil

Shell and devein shrimp, leaving tails intact. Combine juice, gingerroot, sauce, sesame oil and spice in bowl, stir in shrimp; cover, refrigerate 1 hour.

Thread shrimp onto 15 skewers.
Just before serving, heat oil in pan, add skewers, cook until cooked through.

Makes 15.

■ Shrimp can be prepared a day ahead.
■ Storage: Covered, in refrigerator.
■ Freeze: Suitable.
■ Microwave: Not suitable.

GARLIC AND PEPPER QUAIL BREASTS

24 quail breast halves, halved
4 cloves garlic, minced
1½ teaspoons cracked black peppercorns
1 tablespoon vegetable oil
1 tablespoon vegetable oil, extra

Combine quail, garlic, pepper and oil in bowl; cover, refrigerate 1 hour.
Just before serving, heat extra oil in pan, add quail, cook about 2 minutes on each side or until well browned and cooked through. Serve immediately.

Makes 48.

■ Quail can be prepared 2 days ahead.
■ Storage: Covered, in refrigerator.
■ Freeze: Suitable.
■ Microwave: Not suitable.

SESAME CHEESE CROQUETTES

2 eggs
2 cups (½ lb) grated American cheese
⅔ cup grated fresh Parmesan cheese
3 tablespoons all-purpose flour
¼ cup sesame seeds
2 tablespoons chopped fresh chives
2 tablespoons sesame seeds, extra
oil for deep-frying

CRISPY CHICKEN KABOBS WITH SHERRIED CHILI SAUCE

1¼lb chicken thighs, boned, skinned
2 teaspoons grated fresh gingerroot
¼ cup light soy sauce
3 tablespoons dry sherry
cornstarch
oil for shallow-frying

SHERRIED CHILI SAUCE
¼ cup light soy sauce
2 teaspoons dry sherry
1 small fresh red chili pepper, sliced
1 clove garlic, sliced

Cut chicken into thin strips, thread onto 16 skewers. Using 2 spoons, squeeze juice from gingerroot, discard pulp. Combine gingerroot juice, sauce and sherry in bowl, pour over chicken; cover, stand 30 minutes.
Just before serving, toss kabobs in cornstarch, shake away excess cornstarch. Shallow-fry kabobs in hot oil until chicken

is crisp and tender. Serve hot with sauce.
Sherried Chili Sauce: Combine all ingredients in bowl; mix well.

Makes 16.

■ Unfloured kabobs can be prepared a day ahead.
■ Storage: Covered, in refrigerator.
■ Freeze: Unfloured kabobs suitable.
■ Microwave: Not suitable.

BAKED OYSTERS WITH GARLIC HERB BUTTER

24 oysters in half shells
¼ cup (½ stick) butter
2 green onions, chopped
1 clove garlic, minced
2 teaspoons chopped fresh chives
1 teaspoon chopped fresh parsley
1 tablespoon grated fresh Parmesan cheese

Blend or process eggs, cheeses, flour, seeds and chives until combined; cover, refrigerate 30 minutes. Roll 2 level teaspoons of mixture into a croquette, roll in extra seeds. Repeat with remaining mixture and extra seeds.

Just before serving, deep-fry croquettes in hot oil until well browned, drain on absorbent paper.

Makes about 40.

■ Can be prepared 2 days ahead.
■ Storage: Covered, in refrigerator.
■ Freeze: Not suitable.
■ Microwave: Not suitable.

ABOVE LEFT: From left: Crispy Chicken Kabobs with Sherried Chili Sauce, Baked Oysters with Garlic Herb Butter.
ABOVE: From front: Lemon Ginger Shrimp, Sesame Cheese Croquettes, Garlic and Pepper Quail Breasts.

CURRIED CRESCENTS WITH TOMATO SAUCE

4½ cups self-rising flour
3oz (¾ stick) butter
1½ cups milk, approximately
1 egg, lightly beaten
oil for deep-frying

FILLING
1 tablespoon vegetable oil
1 clove garlic, minced
1 small onion, chopped
10oz ground pork and veal
3 tablespoons chopped fresh parsley
2 teaspoons curry powder
3 tablespoons tomato paste
1 tablespoon white vinegar
1 small red bell pepper,
    finely chopped
1 tablespoon all-purpose flour
2 teaspoons water

TOMATO SAUCE
1 tablespoon vegetable oil
1 clove garlic, minced
1 small onion, chopped
14½oz can tomatoes
1 tablespoon tomato paste
2 teaspoons sugar

Sift flour into bowl, rub in butter, stir in enough milk to mix to a firm dough. Knead dough gently on lightly floured surface until smooth. Roll dough on lightly floured surface until ⅛ inch thick, cut into 2¼ inch rounds. Lightly brush rounds with egg, top each round with ¼ level teaspoon of filling. Fold rounds in half, press edges together with fork.

Just before serving, deep-fry crescents in hot oil until lightly browned and cooked through; drain on absorbent paper. Serve crescents hot with sauce.

Filling: Heat oil in pan, add garlic and onion, cook, stirring, until onion is soft. Add pork and veal, cook, stirring, until well browned. Stir in parsley, curry powder, paste, vinegar and pepper. Cook, uncovered, 10 minutes, stir in blended flour and water, stir over heat until mixture boils and thickens; cool.

Tomato Sauce: Heat oil in pan, add garlic and onion, cook, stirring, until onion is soft. Stir in undrained crushed tomatoes, paste and sugar, bring to boil, simmer, uncovered, about 10 minutes or until thick. Blend or process until smooth, strain.

Makes about 60.

■ Crescents and sauce can be
    prepared a day ahead.
■ Storage: Covered, in refrigerator.
■ Freeze: Uncooked crescents suitable.
■ Microwave: Not suitable.

LAMB STICKS WITH HERB YOGURT DIP

1½lb ground lean lamb
1 onion, grated
1 clove garlic, minced
1 teaspoon ground cinnamon
2 teaspoons paprika
2 teaspoons ground cumin
¼ teaspoon chili powder
3 tablespoons chopped
    fresh mint
¼ cup chopped fresh parsley
2 tablespoons dry red wine

HERB YOGURT DIP
2 cups plain yogurt
2 cloves garlic, minced
2 tablespoons chopped
    fresh parsley
3 tablespoons chopped fresh mint
1 tablespoon chopped fresh chives

Combine lamb, onion, garlic, spices, herbs and wine in bowl; mix well. Shape a rounded tablespoon of mixture around 1 end of skewers.
Just before serving, broil sticks until well browned all over and cooked through. Serve hot with dip.
Herb Yogurt Dip: Combine all ingredients in bowl; mix well.

Makes about 40.

■ Sticks and sauce can be prepared a
    day ahead.
■ Storage: Covered, in refrigerator.
■ Freeze: Uncooked sticks suitable.
    Sauce not suitable.
■ Microwave: Not suitable.

ABOVE LEFT: From front: Lamb Sticks with Herb Yogurt Dip, Curried Crescents with Tomato Sauce.
ABOVE RIGHT: Golden Fish Bites.

GOLDEN FISH BITES

½lb boneless white fish fillets
2 green onions, chopped
2 teaspoons light soy sauce
1 egg white
1 teaspoon cornstarch
15 slices fresh white bread
oil for deep-frying

SAUCE
2 teaspoons cornstarch
3 tablespoons lemon juice
1 teaspoon light soy sauce
1 small chicken bouillon cube, crumbled
½ cup water
1 green onion, chopped

Blend or process fish until finely ground. Transfer fish to bowl, stir in onions, sauce, egg white and cornstarch; mix well. Remove crusts from bread, cut bread into ¼ inch cubes. Using damp hands, roll level teaspoons of fish mixture into balls, toss balls in bread cubes, press cubes on firmly; cover, refrigerate 30 minutes.

Just before serving, deep-fry bites in hot oil until lightly browned and cooked through. Serve hot with sauce.

Sauce: Blend cornstarch with juice in pan, stir in remaining ingredients, stir over heat until sauce boils and thickens.

Makes about 40.

■ Bites can be prepared a day ahead.
■ Storage: Covered, in refrigerator.
■ Freeze: Suitable.
■ Microwave: Not suitable.

CHEESE AND VEGETABLE KABOBS IN CURRIED BATTER

10oz broccoli, chopped
10oz cauliflower, chopped
¼lb cheddar cheese, cubed
all-purpose flour
oil for deep-frying

BATTER
1½ cups self-rising flour
2 teaspoons curry powder
¼ teaspoon garam masala
1½ teaspoons sugar
2 eggs, separated
2½ cups milk

YOGURT DIP
1 cup plain yogurt
1 teaspoon chopped fresh chives
⅓ cup chopped walnuts or pecans

Boil, steam or microwave broccoli and cauliflower until just tender, rinse under cold water, drain on absorbent paper. Thread broccoli, cauliflower and cheese onto skewers, toss in flour, shake away excess flour.

Just before serving, dip kabobs in batter, deep-fry in hot oil until lightly browned, drain on absorbent paper. Serve kabobs hot with dip.

Batter: Sift dry ingredients into large bowl, gradually stir in egg yolks and milk, mix to a smooth batter.

Just before serving, whisk egg whites in small bowl until soft peaks form, fold gently into batter.

Yogurt Dip: Combine all ingredients in bowl, mix well.

Makes about 24.

■ Cheese and vegetables can be threaded onto skewers several hours ahead. Batter without egg whites can be prepared several hours ahead.
■ Storage: Both, covered, in refrigerator.
■ Freeze: Not suitable.
■ Microwave: Vegetables suitable.

ABOVE: Cheese and Vegetable Kabobs in Curried Batter.
RIGHT: Mushroom Palmiers.

MUSHROOM PALMIERS

12oz package frozen puff
   pastry, thawed
1 egg, lightly beaten

FILLING
1 tablespoon vegetable oil
1 tablespoon butter
2 cloves garlic, minced
1 onion, finely chopped
½lb mushrooms, finely chopped
1 tablespoon all-purpose flour
2 tablespoons water
3 tablespoons chopped fresh chives

Roll pastry on lightly floured surface to 10 inch x 14 inch rectangle, cut in half lengthways to form 2 rectangles. Spread half the filling over 1 rectangle; repeat with remaining filling and rectangle.

Fold in long sides of each rectangle so they meet in the center, brush along center with some of the egg, fold in half, press lightly; cover, refrigerate 30 minutes. Cut rolls into ½ inch slices, place with cut-side-up on lightly greased baking sheets, bake in 375°F oven about 12 minutes or until well browned. Serve palmiers hot.

Filling: Heat oil and butter in pan, add garlic and onion, cook, stirring, until onion is soft. Stir in mushrooms, cook about 5 minutes or until mushrooms are soft, stirring often. Add flour, stir over heat for 1 minute, gradually stir in water, stir over heat until mixture boils and thickens. Remove from heat; cool. Stir chives into mushroom mixture.

Makes about 30.

■ Palmiers can be made 2 days ahead.
■ Storage: Covered, in refrigerator.
■ Freeze: Not suitable.
■ Microwave: Not suitable.

SHRIMP AND VEGETABLE FRITTERS

7oz cooked shelled small shrimp
1 carrot
6 green onions
2 eggs
1⅔ cups iced water
2 cups all-purpose flour
3½oz bean sprouts
oil for deep-frying

DIPPING SAUCE
3 tablespoons dark soy sauce
2 teaspoons fish sauce
3 tablespoons mirin
2 thin slices fresh gingerroot

Flatten shrimp slightly. Cut carrot into very thin strips about 1½ inches long. Cut onions into 1½ inch lengths.

Lightly whisk eggs in bowl with water. Add sifted flour all at once, stir until just combined; do not beat.

Place 2 shrimp, some carrot, onions and bean sprouts in a heap on a plate, spoon over enough batter to cover, turn heap over, spoon batter over to cover. Using metal spatula, slide heaps into hot oil, deep-fry until lightly browned; drain on absorbent paper. Serve hot with sauce.

Dipping Sauce: Combine sauces, mirin and gingerroot in bowl.

Makes about 30.

■ Fritters can be made 3 hours ahead; re-fry to serve.
■ Storage: Covered, in refrigerator.
■ Freeze: Not suitable.
■ Microwave: Not suitable.

CHICKEN LIVER MORSELS WITH BACON

½lb chicken livers, trimmed
3 tablespoons dark soy sauce
3 tablespoons dry sherry
3 tablespoons lemon juice
1 clove garlic, minced
1 teaspoon grated fresh gingerroot
1 tablespoon vegetable oil
10 thick slices bacon
¾ cup drained canned sliced
    water chestnuts

Cut livers into ¾ inch pieces, combine in bowl with sauce, sherry, juice, garlic and gingerroot; cover, refrigerate 2 hours.

Heat oil in pan, add liver mixture, cook, stirring, about 5 minutes or until livers are lightly browned all over and tender. Drain livers, discard liquid; cool.

Cut each bacon slice into 3 pieces. Wrap a piece of liver and a slice of chestnut in a piece of bacon, secure with a toothpick. Repeat with remaining livers, chestnuts and bacon.

Just before serving, broil morsels until bacon is crisp and lightly browned.

Makes about 30.

■ Liver can be prepared a day ahead.
■ Storage: Covered, in refrigerator.
■ Freeze: Not suitable.
■ Microwave: Not suitable.

ROASTED RED BELL PEPPER AND ONION TARTLETS

1 sheet (10in x 10in) ready rolled
    shortcrust pastry
1 small red bell pepper
3½oz pearl onions, halved
1 clove garlic, halved
1 tablespoon olive oil
2 tablespoons sour cream
1 egg
1 teaspoon chopped fresh basil

Lightly grease 24 x 1½ inch fluted tart pans or mini muffin pans (4 teaspoon capacity).

Cut 24 x 2 inch rounds from pastry, line prepared pans; prick all over with fork. Bake in 375°F oven about 12 minutes or until lightly browned; cool.

Cut pepper into quarters, remove seeds, place quarters with skin-side-up on baking sheet. Place unpeeled onions and unpeeled garlic on baking sheet with pepper. Brush vegetables with oil, bake in 400°F oven about 15 minutes or until pepper skin blisters and browns; cool.

Remove skin from vegetables; chop onions finely. Blend or process pepper, garlic, sour cream, egg and basil until smooth and creamy.

Just before serving, divide onions between pastry cases, top with level teaspoons of pepper mixture. Bake in 375°F oven about 12 minutes or until set. Serve warm.

Makes 24.

■ Cases and filling can be prepared separately a day ahead.
■ Storage: Pastry cases in airtight container. Filling, covered, in refrigerator.
■ Freeze: Not suitable.
■ Microwave: Not suitable.

LEFT: Clockwise from front: Chicken Liver Morsels with Bacon, Shrimp and Vegetable Fritters, Roasted Red Bell Pepper and Onion Tartlets.

SWEET POTATO CUMIN PUFFS

½ cup water
3 tablespoons butter
½ cup all-purpose flour
¼ teaspoon turmeric
2 eggs
2 teaspoons chopped fresh chives
1 egg, lightly beaten, extra

FILLING
½lb sweet potato, chopped
1 medium (3½oz) potato, chopped
1 medium onion, finely grated
½ teaspoon ground cumin
¼ cup sour cream

Combine water and butter in pan, bring to boil, stirring, until butter is melted. Add sifted flour and turmeric all at once, stir vigorously over heat until mixture leaves side of pan and forms a smooth ball.

Transfer mixture to small bowl of electric mixer (or into processor). Add eggs 1 at a time, beat on low speed until smooth after each addition, stir in chives.

Spoon mixture into piping bag fitted with ⅜ inch plain tube, pipe small balls or drop ½ level teaspoons of mixture about ¾ inch apart onto lightly greased baking sheets. Gently brush each ball lightly with extra egg. Bake in 400˚F oven 10 minutes, reduce heat to 350˚F, bake further 5 minutes or until puffs are lightly browned and crisp. Cool on wire rack.

Cut each puff in half. Spoon or pipe filling into each puff base, replace tops, place onto baking sheets.

Just before serving, reheat in 350˚F oven about 5 minutes.

Filling: Boil, steam or microwave sweet potato and potato until tender; drain. Mash well in bowl, stir in onion, cumin and sour cream, stir until well combined.

Makes about 70.

- ■ Puffs and filling can be made separately a day ahead. Puffs can be filled an hour ahead.
- ■ Storage: Unfilled puffs in airtight container. Filling, covered, in refrigerator.
- ■ Freeze: Unfilled puffs suitable.
- ■ Microwave: Filling suitable.

MINI BEEF MIGNONS

¾lb piece beef tenderloin
15 slices prosciutto
3 tablespoons vegetable oil

BEARNAISE SAUCE
⅓ cup white vinegar
6 black peppercorns
1 bay leaf
2 green onions, chopped
2 tablespoons chopped
**   fresh tarragon**
2 egg yolks
1 cup (2 sticks) butter, melted
2 teaspoons chopped fresh
**   tarragon, extra**

Cut beef into ¾ inch pieces. Cut prosciutto in halves lengthways. Wrap a piece of prosciutto around a piece of beef, secure with a toothpick. Repeat with remaining prosciutto and beef.

Just before serving, heat half the oil in pan, add half the beef, cook over high heat until browned all over and tender. Repeat with remaining oil and beef. Serve hot with sauce.

Bearnaise Sauce: Combine vinegar, peppercorns, bay leaf, onions and tarragon in pan, bring to boil, simmer, uncovered, until reduced by half. Strain mixture, reserve liquid.

Blend or process egg yolks and reserved liquid until smooth. Gradually pour in hot bubbling butter while motor is operating, blend until thick and smooth. Stir in extra tarragon.

Makes about 30.

- ■ Mignons can be prepared a day ahead; sauce made an hour ahead.
- ■ Storage: Mignons, covered, in refrigerator. Sauce, covered, at room temperature.
- ■ Freeze: Not suitable.
- ■ Microwave: Not suitable.

MARINATED LAMB RIBLETS

4lb lamb riblets
½ cup ginger wine
½ cup dry white wine
1 cup vegetable oil
3 tablespoons plum sauce
3 cloves garlic, minced
2 teaspoons sugar
3 tablespoons grated fresh gingerroot
2 teaspoons chopped fresh rosemary

Trim 1 inch of meat from the bone at one end of each riblet. Combine riblets in bowl with remaining ingredients; cover, refrigerate overnight.

Just before serving, wrap ends of riblets in foil, broil until well browned and tender.

Makes about 30.

- ■ Riblets can be prepared 2 days ahead.
- ■ Storage: Covered, in refrigerator.
- ■ Freeze: Uncooked riblets suitable.
- ■ Microwave: Not suitable.

LEFT: From front: Sweet Potato Cumin Puffs, Mini Beef Mignons.
BELOW: Marinated Lamb Riblets.

CRISP LITTLE POTATO ROSTI WITH LEMON CHIVE CREAM

2 tablespoons (¼ stick) butter
1 onion, chopped
3 medium (10oz) old potatoes,
    coarsely grated
1 tablespoon butter, extra
1 tablespoon vegetable oil

LEMON CHIVE CREAM
3oz packaged cream cheese
3 tablespoons sour cream
1 teaspoon grated lemon zest
1 tablespoon lemon juice
1 tablespoon chopped
    fresh chives

Heat butter in pan, add onion, cook, stirring, until soft. Add potatoes, stir until potatoes are sticky; cool.

Shape level teaspoons of potato mixture into rounds with wet fingers; flatten slightly. Heat extra butter and oil in pan, add rosti, cook on each side for about 3 minutes or until well browned. Serve warm topped with lemon chive cream and extra chives, if desired.

Lemon Chive Cream: Beat cheese and sour cream in small bowl with wooden spoon until smooth and creamy, beat in zest, juice and chives.

Makes about 40.

■ Rosti can be made 3 hours ahead.
■ Storage: At room temperature.
■ Freeze: Not suitable.
■ Microwave: Not suitable.

CHICKEN AND PIMIENTO BASKETS

2 sheets phyllo pastry
3 tablespoons butter, melted

FILLING
7oz can pimientos, drained, chopped
½ cup chopped cooked chicken
1 tablespoon cornstarch
½ cup heavy cream
1 teaspoon French mustard
2 tablespoons chopped fresh parsley

Cut each sheet of pastry into 8 strips lengthways. Cut each strip into 6 pieces; cover with plastic wrap. Brush 4 rectangles with butter, layer together at angles, place in 1 hole of a mini muffin pan (4 teaspoon capacity). Repeat with remaining rectangles and butter. Bake in 350°F oven about 5 minutes or until lightly browned. Remove pastry baskets from pan, place onto baking sheet.

Just before serving, spoon filling into pastry baskets, bake in 350°F oven about 5 minutes or until heated through.

Filling: Combine pimientos and chicken in pan, stir in blended cornstarch and cream. Stir over heat until mixture boils and thickens, stir in mustard and parsley; cool to room temperature.

Makes 24.

■ Baskets can be baked 2 days ahead. Filling can be prepared 3 hours ahead.
■ Storage: Unfilled baskets, in airtight container. Filling, covered, in refrigerator.
■ Freeze: Not suitable.
■ Microwave: Filling suitable.

SMOKED SALMON AND CAMEMBERT PUFFS

7oz peppered camembert
2 sheets (10in x 10in) ready rolled
puff pastry
3½oz smoked salmon, sliced
½ lime, thinly sliced
fresh dill sprigs

Remove rind from cheese, cut cheese into thin 2 inch squares. Cut 2¼ inch rounds from pastry, place rounds in ungreased 12-hole tart trays, top with cheese.

Just before serving, bake puffs in 350°F oven about 25 minutes or until browned. Remove puffs from trays, top with salmon, lime wedges and dill.

Makes about 30.

■ Tart trays can be lined a day ahead.
■ Storage: Covered, in refrigerator.
■ Freeze: Not suitable.
■ Microwave: Not suitable.

LEFT: Crisp Little Potato Rosti with Lemon Chive Cream.
BELOW: From left: Chicken and Pimiento Baskets, Smoked Salmon and Camembert Puffs.

CHICKEN AND CORN IN CREPE CUPS

½ cup all-purpose flour
2 eggs, lightly beaten
2 teaspoons vegetable oil
½ cup milk
1 tablespoon chopped fresh chives

FILLING
2 tablespoons (¼ stick) butter
¼ teaspoon dry mustard
½ onion, finely chopped
2oz button mushrooms, finely chopped
2 tablespoons all-purpose flour
½ cup milk
1 boneless, skinless chicken breast half, finely chopped
¼ cup canned creamed corn

Sift flour into bowl, gradually stir in combined eggs, oil and milk, beat to a smooth batter (or blend or process all ingredients until smooth); cover, stand 30 minutes.

Pour 3 to 4 tablespoons of batter into heated greased heavy-based crepe pan, cook until lightly browned underneath. Turn crepe, brown on other side. Repeat with remaining batter.

Cut 2¼ inch rounds from crepes.

Just before serving, line mini muffin pans (4 teaspoon capacity) with crepe rounds, bake in 375°F oven 10 minutes. Spoon filling into cases, bake further 5 minutes or until heated through. Sprinkle evenly with chives.

Filling: Heat butter in pan, stir in mustard, onion and mushrooms, cook, stirring, until onion is soft. Stir in flour, cook 1 minute. Remove from heat, gradually stir in milk, chicken and corn, stir over heat until sauce boils and thickens. Simmer, covered, until chicken is tender; cool.

Makes about 55.

■ Cups and filling can be prepared separately 2 days ahead.
■ Storage: Covered, in refrigerator.
■ Freeze: Crepes suitable.
■ Microwave: Filling suitable.

BEEF EN CROUTE WITH GLAZED ONION

1 tablespoon vegetable oil
7oz piece beef tenderloin
1 clove garlic, minced
½ onion, sliced
1 tablespoon honey
5 thick slices white bread
¼ cup (½ stick) butter, melted
1 tablespoon seeded mustard

Heat oil in pan, add beef, cook over high heat on each side until medium rare. Remove beef from pan, stand 5 minutes before slicing thinly. Add garlic and onion to same pan, cook, stirring, until onion is soft. Stir in honey, remove from heat.

Cut 4 x 1¾ inch rounds from each slice of bread. Brush rounds on both sides with butter, place on baking sheet. Bake in 350°F oven about 10 minutes or until lightly browned and crisp.

Just before serving, spread rounds with a little mustard, top with beef and a small amount of onion, place on baking sheet. Bake in 350°F oven about 5 minutes or until heated through.

Makes 20.

■ Croutes can be prepared 2 days ahead. Beef and onion can be prepared 2 hours ahead.
■ Storage: Croutes in airtight container. Beef and onion, covered, in refrigerator.
■ Freeze: Croutes suitable.
■ Microwave: Not suitable.

COCONUT SHRIMP WITH MANGO SAUCE

1lb large uncooked shrimp, shelled
cornstarch
1 egg white, lightly beaten
1 cup (2½oz) shredded coconut
oil for deep-frying

MANGO SAUCE
14oz can mango slices, drained
3 tablespoons mayonnaise
3 tablespoons mango chutney

Toss shrimp in cornstarch, shake away excess cornstarch. Dip shrimp in egg white, then coconut.

Just before serving, deep-fry shrimp in hot oil until lightly browned and tender. Serve hot with sauce.

Mango Sauce: Blend or process mango, mayonnaise and chutney until smooth.

Makes about 18.

■ Shrimp and sauce can be prepared a day ahead.
■ Storage: Both, covered, in refrigerator.
■ Freeze: Not suitable.
■ Microwave: Not suitable.

LEFT: Clockwise from left: Coconut Shrimp with Mango Sauce, Chicken and Corn in Crepe Cups, Beef en Croute with Glazed Onion.

SCALLOP AND BACON BITES

¼ teaspoon ground nutmeg
¼ teaspoon garam masala
½ teaspoon five-spice powder
¼ cup light soy sauce
1 tablespoon vegetable oil
¼ teaspoon sugar
1lb sea scallops
10 thick slices bacon

Combine spices, sauce, oil and sugar in bowl, stir in scallops; cover, refrigerate several hours.

Cut each bacon slice crossways into 3 pieces, wrap scallops in bacon pieces, secure with toothpicks.

Just before serving, broil bites until bacon is lightly browned.

Makes about 30.

■ Bites can be prepared a day ahead.
■ Storage: Covered, in refrigerator.
■ Freeze: Not suitable.
■ Microwave: Not suitable.

GARLIC CHICKEN KABOBS

**1½lb boneless, skinless chicken
  breast halves**
½ cup light soy sauce
1 teaspoon grated lemon zest
¼ cup lemon juice
2 tablespoons sugar
3 tablespoons vegetable oil
CREAMY GARLIC SAUCE
½ cup heavy cream
½ cup sour cream
2 cloves garlic, minced

Cut chicken into ¾ inch pieces, combine
in bowl with sauce, zest, juice, sugar and
oil; cover, refrigerate 2 hours.
    Thread chicken onto skewers.
Just before serving, broil kabobs until
chicken is lightly browned and tender,
serve hot with hot sauce.
Creamy Garlic Sauce: Combine all ingredients in pan, bring to boil, simmer, uncovered,
about 5 minutes or until slightly thickened.

Makes about 15.

■ Kabobs can be prepared a day ahead.
■ Storage: Covered, in refrigerator.
■ Freeze: Uncooked chicken suitable.
■ Microwave: Sauce suitable.

SWEET POTATO AND
SESAME FINGERS

*You will need about 1½lb sweet potato
for this recipe.*

3 eggs
¼ cup fresh orange juice
¼ cup sour cream
2 teaspoons chopped fresh chives
¼ teaspoon ground cinnamon
¼ teaspoon ground cumin
**2 cups cooked mashed
  sweet potato**
1 tablespoon sesame seeds

Lightly grease 8 inch x 12 inch baking pan,
place strip of baking paper to cover base
and extend over 2 opposite sides.
    Whisk eggs until combined, whisk in juice,
cream, chives, spices and sweet potato.
Pour mixture into prepared pan, sprinkle
evenly with seeds. Bake in 350°F oven about
20 minutes or until firm. Cut while hot.

Makes about 50.

■ Slice can be made a day ahead.
■ Storage: Covered, in refrigerator.
■ Freeze: Not suitable.
■ Microwave: Not suitable.

CRUNCHY POTATO SKINS
WITH SOUR CREAM

4 large potatoes
3 tablespoons vegetable oil
1 teaspoon dry mustard
1 teaspoon seasoned pepper
8oz container sour cream

Scrub potatoes, bake in 400°F oven about
50 minutes or until cooked through. Cut
potatoes into eighths, scoop out flesh
carefully, leaving skins intact (reserve
flesh for another recipe).

Combine oil, mustard and pepper,
brush over potato skins, place on baking
sheet with skin-side-up.
Just before serving, bake skins in 400°F
oven about 10 minutes or until crisp.
Serve hot with sour cream. Serve
sprinkled with coarse sea salt, if desired.
Makes 32.

■ Skins can be prepared for cooking
  a day ahead.
■ Storage: Covered, in refrigerator.
■ Freeze: Not suitable.
■ Microwave: Not suitable.

*LEFT: Clockwise from front: Sweet Potato
and Sesame Fingers, Scallop and Bacon
Bites, Garlic Chicken Kabobs.
ABOVE: Crunchy Potato Skins with
Sour Cream.*

SPICED FISH NIBBLES

10oz boneless white fish
  fillets, skinned
½ cup packaged unseasoned
  bread crumbs
1 egg
1 teaspoon grated fresh gingerroot
¼ teaspoon chili powder
1 tablespoon ground coriander
oil for deep-frying

Blend or process fish, bread crumbs, egg, gingerroot and spices until mixture forms a ball. Roll 2 level teaspoons of mixture into a ball; repeat with remaining mixture.

Just before serving, deep-fry nibbles in hot oil until lightly browned and cooked through. Serve hot, drizzled with lemon juice, if desired.

Makes about 30.

■ Nibbles can be prepared a day ahead.
■ Storage: Covered, in refrigerator.
■ Freeze: Uncooked nibbles suitable.
■ Microwave: Not suitable.

CHICKEN AND RED BELL PEPPER PASTIES

1 cup self-rising flour
3 cups all-purpose flour
1 cup (2 sticks) butter
2 egg yolks, lightly beaten
½ cup water, approximately
1 egg, lightly beaten
paprika

FILLING
1 tablespoon butter
1 tablespoon vegetable oil
2 onions, chopped
1¼lb chicken thighs, boned,
  skinned, chopped
1 tablespoon French mustard
½ red bell pepper, finely chopped

Sift flours into bowl, rub in butter. Stir in egg yolks with enough water to mix to a firm dough. Knead dough on floured surface until smooth; cover, refrigerate 30 minutes.

Cut pastry in half, roll each half on lightly floured surface until ⅛ inch thick. Cut into 3½ inch rounds, top each round with 2 level teaspoons of filling. Lightly brush edges with water, fold in half, press edges together to seal. Place pasties, standing upright, onto lightly greased baking sheets, brush with egg, sprinkle pasties with paprika.

Just before serving, bake pasties in 375°F oven about 20 minutes or until well browned.

Filling: Heat butter and oil in pan, add onions, cook, stirring, until onions are soft. Add chicken, cook for about 5 minutes or until cooked. Blend or process mixture until chicken is finely chopped, transfer mixture to bowl, stir in mustard and pepper.

Makes about 45.

■ Pasties can be prepared a day ahead.
■ Storage: Covered, in refrigerator.
■ Freeze: Uncooked pasties suitable.
■ Microwave: Not suitable.

MINI PIZZA SWIRLS

1 teaspoon sugar
1 package (¼oz) active dry yeast
¼ cup warm water
1½ cups all-purpose flour
1 teaspoon salt
1 tablespoon vegetable oil
½ cup warm water,
  extra, approximately

TOMATO SAUCE
1 teaspoon vegetable oil
1 clove garlic, minced
½ cup tomato paste
3 tablespoons tomato sauce
1 teaspoon dried oregano leaves

TOPPING
1 small onion, finely chopped
½ small green bell pepper,
  finely chopped
2 hard-boiled eggs, chopped
⅓ cup shredded mozzarella cheese

Combine sugar, yeast and water in bowl; cover, stand in warm place about 10 minutes or until foamy.

Sift flour and salt into bowl, stir in yeast mixture, oil, and enough extra water to mix to a soft dough. Knead dough on lightly floured surface 10 minutes. Place dough in lightly oiled bowl; cover, stand in warm place about 45 minutes or until dough is doubled in size.

Knead dough on lightly floured surface until smooth. Roll half the dough to an 8 inch x 15 inch rectangle, spread with half the tomato sauce, sprinkle with half the topping. Roll up tightly from long side, cut into ½ inch slices, place slices cut-side-up on greased baking sheets. Repeat with remaining dough, tomato sauce and topping. Bake in 350°F oven about 15 minutes or until well browned. Serve swirls hot.

Tomato Sauce: Heat oil in pan, add garlic, cook 1 minute, stir in paste, sauce and oregano; cool.

Topping: Combine all ingredients in bowl.

Makes about 60.

■ Swirls can be made 3 hours ahead.
■ Storage: At room temperature.
■ Freeze: Cooked swirls suitable.
■ Microwave: Tomato sauce suitable.

RIGHT: From left: Spiced Fish Nibbles, Chicken and Red Bell Pepper Pasties, Mini Pizza Swirls.

HOT EGG DIP WITH SALAMI STICKS

4oz package cream cheese
¼ cup sour cream
¼ cup mayonnaise
1 tablespoon chopped
    fresh chives
1 teaspoon seeded mustard
6 hard-boiled eggs, chopped

SALAMI STICKS
28in French bread stick
¾ cup (1½ sticks) butter
3½oz salami, chopped
1 tablespoon chopped fresh chives
1½ cups (6oz) grated
    cheddar cheese

Beat cream cheese in bowl until smooth, beat in sour cream, mayonnaise, chives and mustard, stir in eggs.

Just before serving, place egg mixture in pan, stir over low heat until warm; do not boil. Serve with hot salami sticks.
Salami Sticks: Cut bread stick in half crossways, split in halves lengthways. Beat butter in bowl until smooth, stir in salami and chives. Spread mixture evenly over bread, sprinkle with cheese, press cheese on firmly.
Just before serving, broil bread until cheese is melted. Cut bread into chunks.

Makes about 2 cups dip.

■ Dip and salami sticks can be prepared a day ahead.
■ Storage: Both, covered, in refrigerator.
■ Freeze: Salami sticks suitable.
■ Microwave: Not suitable.

SWEET POTATO SCONES WITH CREAMY HERB CHEESE

1 medium (¾lb) sweet potato
2 cups self-rising flour
2 teaspoons sugar
1 tablespoon butter
1 cup milk, approximately

CREAMY HERB CHEESE
5oz packaged cream cheese
3 tablespoons chopped
    fresh parsley
1 tablespoon chopped
    fresh chives

Lightly grease 9 inch square baking pan. Place potato on baking sheet, pierce with fork, bake in 350°F oven about 45 minutes or until tender; cool to room temperature. Peel and mash potato (you will need 1 cup of mashed potato).

Sift flour and sugar into bowl; rub in butter. Stir in potato and enough milk to mix to a soft dough. Turn dough onto lightly floured surface, knead gently until smooth. Press dough evenly on lightly floured surface until ½ inch thick; cut into 1¾ inch rounds. Place scones in prepared pan; brush tops lightly with a little extra milk.
Just before serving, bake scones in 450°F oven about 15 minutes or until tops are browned. Split scones in half, sandwich with herb cheese.
Creamy Herb Cheese: Beat cheese in small bowl with electric mixer until light and fluffy, stir in herbs.

Makes about 36.

■ Scones and herb cheese can be made 3 hours ahead.
■ Storage: Scones, covered, at room temperature. Herb cheese, covered, in refrigerator.
■ Freeze: Scones suitable.
■ Microwave: Not suitable.

CHICKEN AND GREEN ONION ROLLS

½lb chicken thighs, boned, skinned
5 green onions
1 tablespoon grated
    fresh gingerroot
¼ cup dry sherry
⅓ cup light soy sauce
1½ tablespoons dark brown sugar
30 egg pastry sheets
oil for deep-frying

SAUCE
2 green onions, finely sliced

Cut chicken into ½ inch strips. Cut onions into 1¾ inch lengths, then halve lengthways. Combine chicken, onions, gingerroot, sherry, sauce and sugar in bowl; cover, refrigerate 30 minutes.

Drain chicken and onions; reserve marinade for sauce.

Lightly brush an edge of a pastry sheet with water. Place a piece of chicken and a few strips of onion at opposite end, fold in sides, then roll up, pressing moistened

end to seal. Repeat with remaining pastry, chicken and onions.

Just before serving, deep-fry rolls in hot oil until well browned; drain on absorbent paper. Serve warm with sauce.

Sauce: Heat reserved marinade in pan, bring to boil, stir in onions.

Makes 30.

■ Rolls can be made a day ahead.
■ Storage: Egg rolls and sauce, covered, in refrigerator.
■ Freeze: Uncooked egg rolls suitable.
■ Microwave: Sauce suitable.

LEFT: Hot Egg Dip with Salami Sticks.
ABOVE: From back: Sweet Potato Scones with Creamy Herb Cheese, Chicken and Green Onion Rolls.

SPICY BEEF PUFFS WITH TOMATO SAUCE

½lb ground beef
3 green onions, finely chopped
3 tablespoons chopped fresh parsley
¼ teaspoon garam masala
¼ teaspoon five-spice powder
¼ teaspoon dry mustard
1 tablespoon tomato paste
½ cup grated cheddar cheese
3 sheets (10in x 10in) ready rolled
　　shortcrust pastry
oil for deep-frying

TOMATO SAUCE
10oz can Tomato Supreme
¼ teaspoon seasoned pepper
1 teaspoon Worcestershire sauce
½ teaspoon dry mustard
2 tablespoons chopped fresh chives

Cook beef in pan over high heat, stirring, until beef is browned and cooked. Stir in onions, parsley, spices and paste, stir over heat until all liquid has evaporated. Remove from heat, stir in cheese.

Cut pastry into 2¼ inch rounds, top each round with 1 level teaspoon of mixture, lightly brush edges with water, fold in half, press edges together.

Just before serving, deep-fry puffs in hot oil until well browned; drain on absorbent paper. Serve hot with sauce.

Tomato Sauce: Combine Tomato Supreme, pepper, sauce, mustard and chives in pan, bring to boil.

Makes about 40.

■ Both can be prepared a day ahead.
■ Storage: Both, covered, in refrigerator.
■ Freeze: Uncooked puffs suitable.
■ Microwave: Sauce suitable.

SMOKED TURKEY PUMPERNICKEL CANAPES

¼lb smoked turkey, finely chopped
2 tablespoons sour cream
2 teaspoons horseradish cream
1 teaspoon chopped fresh chives
½lb sliced pumpernickel rounds
3½oz Swiss cheese, thinly sliced

Combine turkey, sour cream, horseradish cream and chives in bowl. Place 1 level teaspoon of mixture onto each pumpernickel round, place rounds on baking paper-lined baking sheets. Cut cheese into pieces large enough to cover rounds, place on top of turkey mixture.

Just before serving, bake canapes in 400°F oven until cheese is bubbling.

Makes about 24.

■ Canapes can be prepared several
　　hours ahead.
■ Storage: Covered, in refrigerator.
■ Freeze: Not suitable.
■ Microwave: Not suitable.

CHEESY TOMATO BASIL MUSSELS

35 (3lb) small mussels
½ cup dry white wine
3 tablespoons butter
1 onion, finely chopped
2 cloves garlic, minced
14½oz can tomatoes
3 tablespoons chopped fresh basil
2oz gruyere cheese, grated

Scrub mussels, remove beards. Heat wine in large pan, add mussels, cook, covered, over high heat about 5 minutes or until mussels open. Drain; discard liquid. Place each mussel in half a shell, place on baking sheet.

Heat butter in pan, add onion and garlic, cook, stirring, until onion is soft. Stir in undrained crushed tomatoes, bring to boil, simmer, uncovered, about 10 minutes or until thickened; stir in basil. Spoon mixture over mussels, sprinkle with cheese.

Just before serving, broil mussels until cheese is lightly browned.

Makes 35.

■ Can be prepared 3 hours ahead.
■ Storage: Covered, in refrigerator.
■ Freeze: Not suitable.
■ Microwave: Not suitable.

RIGHT: Clockwise from back: Spicy Beef Puffs with Tomato Sauce, Cheesy Tomato Basil Mussels, Smoked Turkey Pumpernickel Canapes.

SPINACH AND CHICKEN PINWHEELS

½ bunch (10oz) spinach
3 tablespoons vegetable oil

CREPES
¾ cup all-purpose flour
2 eggs, lightly beaten
¾ cup milk
2 teaspoons vegetable oil

FILLING
1 tablespoon butter
2 green onions, chopped
2 teaspoons drained green
   peppercorns, crushed
10oz ground chicken
1 egg white, lightly beaten
½ cup fresh bread crumbs

Boil, steam or microwave spinach until tender, drain well; cool.

Place 2 crepes end to end, slightly overlapping. Repeat with remaining crepes. Divide filling between crepes, spread filling evenly, cover filling with spinach leaves. Roll crepes up firmly from narrow ends like a jelly roll; cover, refrigerate 30 minutes.

Just before serving, cut ends from rolls; discard ends. Cut each roll into ½ inch slices, place a toothpick through center of each slice.

Heat half the oil in pan, cook half the pinwheels until lightly browned on both sides and filling is cooked through, drain on absorbent paper. Repeat with remaining oil and pinwheels.

Crepes: Sift flour into bowl, gradually stir in combined eggs, milk and oil, mix to a smooth batter (or blend or process until smooth); cover, stand 30 minutes.

Pour 3 to 4 tablespoons of batter into heated greased heavy-based crepe pan; cook until lightly browned underneath. Turn crepe, brown on other side. Repeat with remaining batter. You will need 10 crepes for this recipe.

Filling: Heat butter in pan, stir in onions and peppercorns, cook, stirring, until onions are soft; cool. Combine chicken, egg white, bread crumbs and onion mixture in bowl.

Makes about 50.

■ Rolls can be prepared 2 days ahead.
■ Storage: Covered, in refrigerator.
■ Freeze: Uncooked rolls suitable.
■ Microwave: Filling suitable.

NUTTY BEEF SATAYS

1½lb piece rump steak
½ cup chunky peanut butter
1 small chicken bouillon
   cube, crumbled
1 cup water
3 tablespoons dry sherry
3 tablespoons honey
1 tablespoon dark soy sauce
1 tablespoon lime juice
2 teaspoons curry powder
1 teaspoon grated fresh gingerroot
1 teaspoon ground cumin
1 teaspoon ground coriander

Cut steak into ¾ inch cubes. Thread cubes onto 20 small skewers, place in single layer in shallow dish.

Combine remaining ingredients in bowl, pour over satay sticks; cover, refrigerate several hours or overnight.

Just before serving, drain satay sticks, reserve marinade. Bring marinade to boil in pan, boil, uncovered, about 10 minutes, stirring frequently, or until thickened. Broil satay sticks until beef is cooked. Serve with sauce.

Makes 20.

■ Sticks can be prepared 2 days ahead.
■ Storage: Covered, in refrigerator.
■ Freeze: Uncooked sticks suitable.
■ Microwave: Not suitable.

LEFT: From left: Nutty Beef Satays, Spinach and Chicken Pinwheels.

CHEESY MINI BURGERS

6 slices bread
¼ cup (½ stick) butter, melted
2 tablespoons tomato paste
⅓ cup grated cheddar cheese

MEAT PATTIES
½lb ground beef
1 small onion, finely chopped
½ teaspoon French mustard
½ teaspoon tomato sauce
½ teaspoon Worcestershire sauce
1 tablespoon vegetable oil

Cut 4 x 1¾ inch rounds from each slice of bread. Brush rounds with butter, place on baking sheets, bake in 350°F oven about 15 minutes or until lightly browned and crisp. Spread each round with tomato paste, top with a meat patty and cheese.
Just before serving, broil burgers until cheese is melted.
Meat Patties: Combine beef, onion, mustard and sauces in bowl. Shape 2 level teaspoons of mixture into a ball, flatten to a 1½ inch patty. Repeat with remaining mixture. Heat vegetable oil in pan, add patties, cook until well browned; drain on absorbent paper.

Makes about 24.

■ Patties and bread rounds can be prepared a day ahead.
■ Storage: Patties, covered, in refrigerator.
■ Freeze: Uncooked patties suitable.
■ Microwave: Not suitable.

MUSHROOM CREAM PASTRIES

1 sheet (10in x 10in) ready rolled puff pastry
⅓ cup sour cream
¼ cup grated gruyere cheese
1 teaspoon seeded mustard
¼lb button mushrooms, sliced
1 tablespoon butter, melted
¼ cup grated gruyere cheese, extra

Spread pastry with combined sour cream, cheese and mustard. Cut pastry in halves, arrange mushrooms down center of each half. Fold in long sides over mushrooms. Brush pastry with butter, cut into ¾ inch slices. Place slices on greased baking sheets, sprinkle with extra cheese.
Just before serving, bake pastries in 375°F oven about 15 minutes or until lightly browned. Serve hot.

Makes about 25.

■ Can be prepared 3 hours ahead.
■ Storage: Covered, in refrigerator.
■ Freeze: Not suitable.
■ Microwave: Not suitable.

STEAMED CHILI SHRIMP

1 large (7oz) carrot
45 (2lb) medium uncooked shrimp, shelled
1 tablespoon honey
2 small fresh red chili peppers, chopped
¼ cup vegetable oil

Peel carrot into thin strips using vegetable peeler. Wrap a strip of carrot around each shrimp, secure with toothpicks. Combine honey, chilies and oil in bowl, add shrimp, mix well; cover, refrigerate 1 hour.
Just before serving, place shrimp in steamer in single layer; cover, steam until shrimp are cooked.

Makes 45.

■ Shrimp can be prepared a day ahead.
■ Storage: Covered, in refrigerator.
■ Freeze: Not suitable.
■ Microwave: Suitable.

ABOVE: Cheesy Mini Burgers.
RIGHT: From top: Mushroom Cream Pastries, Steamed Chili Shrimp.

FRESH ASPARAGUS AND SALMON PASTRIES

12oz package frozen puff
   pastry, thawed
¼ cup (½ stick) butter, melted
3 tablespoons vegetable oil
8 medium spears fresh
   asparagus, chopped
1 clove garlic, minced
1 teaspoon grated fresh gingerroot
3 green onions, chopped
1 tablespoon dry sherry
2 teaspoons light soy sauce
1 tablespoon oyster-flavored sauce
½ cup water
1 small chicken bouillon
   cube, crumbled
2 teaspoons cornstarch
2 teaspoons water, extra
7oz can salmon, drained, flaked

Roll pastry on lightly floured surface until ¼ inch thick. Cut 1¾ inch squares from pastry. Using 1¼ inch square cutter, cut three-quarters through squares to make a border around edges. Place squares on baking sheet, brush tops with butter, bake in 375°F oven about 12 minutes or until lightly browned. Remove and discard centers of squares.

Heat oil in pan, add asparagus, garlic and gingerroot, cook, stirring, 5 minutes. Stir in onions, sherry and sauces, then water and bouillon cube, bring to boil, simmer, uncovered, 3 minutes. Stir in blended cornstarch and extra water, stir until mixture boils and thickens. Stir in salmon; cool to room temperature.

Just before serving, spoon salmon mixture into pastry cases, place on baking sheets, reheat in 350°F oven 10 minutes.

Makes about 35.

■ Pastry cases and filling can be made separately a day ahead.
■ Storage: Pastry cases in airtight container. Filling, covered, in refrigerator.
■ Freeze: Pastry cases suitable.
■ Microwave: Not suitable.

LENTIL PIKELETS WITH LEEK AND MUSHROOM TOPPING

⅓ cup brown lentils
1 cup whole-wheat flour
2 teaspoons double-acting
   baking powder
1 egg
¾ cup milk
3 tablespoons olive oil
½ teaspoon ground caraway

LEEK AND MUSHROOM TOPPING
¼ cup (½ stick) butter
1 small leek, sliced
2 cloves garlic, minced
½lb button mushrooms, sliced
10oz jar sweet red bell peppers,
   drained, chopped
3 tablespoons chopped fresh
   tarragon

Add lentils to pan of boiling water, boil, uncovered, about 15 minutes or until just tender; drain.

Blend or process flour, baking powder, egg, milk, oil and caraway until smooth, stir in lentils. Drop level teaspoons of batter into heated non-stick pan, cook until bubbles appear; turn pikelets, brown other side.

Just before serving, top warm pikelets with hot topping.

Leek and Mushroom Topping: Heat butter in pan, add leek, cook over low heat about 10 minutes. Add garlic and mushrooms, cook, stirring, until mushrooms are soft. Stir in peppers and tarragon; mix well.

Makes about 80.

■ Pikelets can be made 3 hours ahead, reheat in oven. Topping can be made 1 hour ahead, reheat before serving.
■ Storage: Pikelets, in airtight container. Topping, at room temperature.
■ Freeze: Cooked pikelets suitable.
■ Microwave: Topping suitable.

RIGHT: From left: Lentil Pikelets with Leek and Mushroom Topping, Fresh Asparagus and Salmon Pastries.

BACON AND EGG RAVIOLI WITH BASIL SAUCE

1⅓ cups all-purpose flour
2 eggs, lightly beaten
2 tablespoons water, approximately
1 egg, lightly beaten, extra
oil for deep-frying

FILLING
1 teaspoon vegetable oil
1 small onion, finely chopped
1 slice bacon, finely chopped
1 hard-boiled egg, finely chopped
1 teaspoon chopped fresh parsley

SAUCE
1 tablespoon butter
1 tablespoon all-purpose flour
1¼ cups milk
1 tablespoon heavy cream
2 teaspoons chopped fresh basil

Sift flour into bowl, stir in eggs with enough water to mix to a firm dough. Knead dough on lightly floured surface until smooth; cover, refrigerate 30 minutes. Roll dough on lightly floured surface until ⅛ inch thick (or follow pasta machine instructions).

Cut 3 inch rounds from dough, cut rounds in half. Lightly brush semi-circles with extra egg, top each semi-circle with ½ level teaspoon of filling, fold in half, press edges together with a fork.

Add ravioli to large pan of boiling water, boil, uncovered, 5 minutes, drain; pat dry with absorbent paper.

Just before serving, deep-fry ravioli in hot oil until lightly browned; drain on absorbent paper. Serve ravioli hot with warm sauce.

Filling: Heat oil in pan, add onion and bacon, cook, stirring, until onion is soft; drain on absorbent paper. Combine onion mixture, egg and parsley in bowl; cool.

Sauce: Heat butter in pan, add flour, cook, stirring, until bubbling. Remove from heat, stir in milk and cream, stir over heat until sauce boils and thickens; stir in basil.

Makes about 40.

■ Ravioli can be prepared a day ahead; sauce several hours ahead.
■ Storage: Both, covered, in refrigerator.
■ Freeze: Ravioli suitable before or after it has been boiled.
■ Microwave: Sauce suitable.

MARINATED BEEF FRITTERS

2 (13oz) beef tenderloin steaks
2 tablespoons oyster-flavored sauce
3 tablespoons light soy sauce
1 tablespoon dry sherry
1 small fresh red chili
    pepper, chopped
½ cup self-rising flour
1 teaspoon paprika
½ cup water
oil for deep-frying
¼ teaspoon cornstarch

Trim fat from steaks, cut steaks into ¾ inch cubes, combine with sauces, sherry and chili in bowl; cover, refrigerate several hours or overnight.

Sift flour and paprika into bowl, gradually stir in water, mix to a smooth batter (or blend or process all ingredients).

Just before serving, drain steak; reserve marinade. Dip pieces of steak into batter, deep-fry in hot oil until lightly browned and tender; drain on absorbent paper. Blend reserved marinade and cornstarch in pan, stir over heat until sauce boils and thickens. Serve fritters hot with hot sauce.

Makes about 25.

- Steak can be prepared a day ahead. Batter can be prepared 1 hour ahead.
- Storage: Both, covered, in refrigerator.
- Freeze: Uncooked steak suitable.
- Microwave: Sauce suitable.

BEEF AND HORSERADISH BONBONS

4 slices (¼lb) sliced roast beef
4 sheets phyllo pastry
¼ cup (½ stick) butter, melted
2 teaspoons chopped fresh parsley
2 teaspoons chopped fresh chives
2 tablespoons horseradish cream

Cut each beef slice into 8 strips. Brush a sheet of pastry with combined butter, parsley, chives and horseradish, top with another pastry sheet, brush with more butter mixture. Cut pastry into quarters, cut each quarter into quarters again.

Top each quarter with a strip of beef, roll up from narrow sides, pinch ends to form bonbon shapes. Repeat with remaining pastry, butter mixture and beef. Place bonbons on lightly greased baking sheets.

Just before serving, bake bonbons in 400°F oven about 8 minutes or until lightly browned and crisp.

Makes 32.

- Bonbons can be prepared a day ahead.
- Storage: Covered, in refrigerator.
- Freeze: Uncooked bonbons suitable.
- Microwave: Not suitable.

ABOVE LEFT: From back: Marinated Beef Fritters, Bacon and Egg Ravioli with Basil Sauce.
ABOVE RIGHT: From top: Creamy Egg and Chive Croquettes, Beef and Horseradish Bonbons.

CREAMY EGG AND CHIVE CROQUETTES

3 tablespoons butter
1 onion, finely chopped
⅓ cup all-purpose flour
1 cup milk
3 tablespoons chopped fresh chives
5 hard-boiled eggs, chopped
3 tablespoons sour cream
2 teaspoons chopped fresh thyme
5 cups (¾lb) fresh bread crumbs
3 eggs, lightly beaten
2 tablespoons milk, extra
oil for deep-frying

Heat butter in pan, add onion, cook, stirring, until soft. Stir in flour, cook until bubbling. Remove from heat, gradually stir in milk. Stir over heat until mixture boils and thickens; cool. Stir in chives, eggs, sour cream and thyme.

Shape rounded tablespoons of mixture into croquettes, roll in bread crumbs, dip in combined eggs and extra milk, then bread crumbs again.

Just before serving, deep-fry croquettes in hot oil until golden brown; drain on absorbent paper.

Makes about 30.

- Can be prepared a day ahead.
- Storage: Covered, in refrigerator.
- Freeze: Cooked croquettes suitable.
- Microwave: Not suitable.

CHICKEN GINGER ROLLS

1½ cups all-purpose flour
1 egg yolk
2oz lard
⅓ cup water
1 egg, lightly beaten
2 teaspoons rock salt

FILLING
½lb ground chicken
1 egg white
1 small onion, grated
3 tablespoons chopped
glace gingerroot
½ cup fresh bread crumbs
3 tablespoons chopped fresh chives

Sift flour into bowl, add egg yolk, cover with some of the flour. Place lard and water into pan, stir over low heat until lard is melted, bring to boil. Pour boiling liquid into flour all at once, mix to a firm dough. Turn dough onto lightly floured surface; knead until smooth; cover, stand 10 minutes.

Divide dough into 2 portions, roll each portion on lightly floured surface into 4¾ inch x 12 inch rectangle. Place half the filling down center of 1 rectangle, brush edges with some of the egg. Fold edges over to cover filling. Repeat with remaining rectangle, filling and more egg.

Place rolls seam-side-down on lightly greased baking sheet. Brush rolls with egg, sprinkle lightly with salt. Bake in 375°F oven about 25 minutes or until well browned. Stand rolls 5 minutes before slicing. Serve hot.

Filling: Combine all ingredients in bowl.

Makes about 60.

■ Rolls can be made a day ahead.
■ Storage: Covered, in refrigerator.
■ Freeze: Cooked rolls suitable.
■ Microwave: Not suitable.

CHEESY PASTRAMI PUFFS

3 tablespoons butter
½ cup water
½ cup all-purpose flour
2 eggs, lightly beaten
¼ cup grated fresh Parmesan cheese

FILLING
¼ cup (½ stick) butter
2 green onions, chopped
1 red bell pepper, finely chopped
¼ cup all-purpose flour
1 cup milk
5 slices (2oz) pastrami,
finely chopped
½ teaspoon paprika

Combine butter and water in pan, bring to boil, stirring, until butter is melted. Stir in sifted flour all at once, stir vigorously over heat until mixture leaves side of pan and forms a smooth ball. Transfer mixture to small bowl of electric mixer (or food processor). Add eggs gradually, beating

well between each addition; beat in cheese. Spoon level teaspoons of mixture onto greased baking sheets, bake in 375°F oven 12 minutes, reduce heat to 350°F, bake further 5 minutes or until lightly browned and crisp. Cut puffs in half, turn oven off; leave puffs to dry out in oven.

Just before serving, join puffs with filling, place on baking sheet, reheat in 350°F oven about 5 minutes.

Filling: Heat butter in pan, add onions and pepper, cook, stirring, until pepper is soft. Stir in flour, stir until bubbling. Remove from heat, gradually stir in milk, then pastrami and paprika. Stir over heat until mixture boils and thickens.

Makes about 65.

- Puffs and filling can be made separately a day ahead.
- Storage: Puffs, in airtight container. Filling, covered, in refrigerator.
- Freeze: Unfilled puffs suitable.
- Microwave: Filling suitable.

CRUMBED CHEESE CUBES

Leyden is a firm, caraway-flavored cheese with a texture similar to cheddar.

5oz Leyden cheese
all-purpose flour
1 egg, lightly beaten
2 tablespoons milk
¾ cup crushed nuts
¼ cup packaged unseasoned bread crumbs
oil for deep-frying

Cut cheese into ½ inch cubes, toss in flour, shake away excess flour. Dip cubes in combined egg and milk, then combined nuts and bread crumbs. Repeat with egg mixture then nut mixture; cover, refrigerate 30 minutes.

Just before serving, deep-fry cubes in hot oil until well browned, drain on absorbent paper. Serve hot.

Makes about 35.

- Cubes can be prepared a day ahead.
- Storage: Covered, in refrigerator.
- Freeze: Not suitable.
- Microwave: Not suitable.

QUAIL SCOTCH EGGS

12 quail eggs
9oz ground chicken
2 tablespoons chopped fresh parsley
2 tablespoons chopped fresh chives
1 teaspoon dry mustard
all-purpose flour
1 egg, lightly beaten
packaged unseasoned bread crumbs
oil for deep-frying

Place eggs in pan, barely cover with cold water, bring to boil, stirring gently to center yolks. Simmer for 4 minutes, drain, place eggs in cold water, crack shells gently; cool to room temperature.

Combine chicken, herbs and mustard in bowl. Divide mixture into 12 portions.

Drain eggs, discard shells. Toss eggs in flour, shake away excess flour. Shape each portion of chicken mixture around each egg, using lightly floured hands. Dip each egg in beaten egg, then into bread crumbs to coat.

Just before serving, deep-fry eggs in hot oil until well browned; drain on absorbent paper. Cut eggs in halves.

Makes 24.

- Eggs can be prepared a day ahead.
- Storage: Covered, in refrigerator.
- Freeze: Not suitable.
- Microwave: Not suitable.

ABOVE LEFT: From back: Chicken Ginger Rolls, Cheesy Pastrami Puffs, Crumbed Cheese Cubes.
ABOVE: Quail Scotch Eggs.

Combine steak, sauce and mustard in bowl; cover, refrigerate 30 minutes.

Cut asparagus and pepper into 2 inch strips. Boil, steam or microwave asparagus and pepper until just tender; drain. Wrap a piece of steak around a piece each of asparagus and pepper, secure with toothpick. Repeat with remaining steak, asparagus and pepper. **Just before serving,** heat oil in pan, add rolls, cook until well browned all over.

Makes about 48.

■ Rolls can be prepared a day ahead.
■ Storage: Covered, in refrigerator.
■ Freeze: Uncooked rolls suitable.
■ Microwave: Not suitable.

CRUMBED SQUID WITH COCONUT CURRY SAUCE

7oz package cheese-flavored corn chips
7oz small cleaned squid, thinly sliced
⅓ cup cornstarch
1 egg, lightly beaten
1 tablespoon milk
oil for deep-frying

COCONUT CURRY SAUCE
1 teaspoon vegetable oil
1 clove garlic, minced
2 teaspoons curry powder
½ teaspoon turmeric
2 teaspoons cornstarch
1 cup canned unsweetened coconut cream
½ teaspoon sugar

Blend or process corn chips until coarsely crushed. Toss squid in cornstarch, shake away excess cornstarch. Dip squid in combined egg and milk, then corn chips, pressing corn chips on firmly; cover, refrigerate 1 hour.

Just before serving, deep-fry squid in hot oil about 30 seconds or until lightly browned. Drain on absorbent paper, serve hot with hot sauce.

Coconut Curry Sauce: Heat oil in pan, add garlic, curry powder and turmeric, cook, stirring, 2 minutes; remove from heat. Blend cornstarch with 1 tablespoon of the coconut cream, stir into curry mixture with sugar. Gradually stir in remaining cream, stir until mixture boils and thickens; simmer 1 minute.

Makes about 50.

■ Squid can be prepared a day ahead. Sauce can be made 1 hour ahead.
■ Storage: Squid, covered, in refrigerator. Sauce, covered, at room temperature.
■ Freeze: Uncooked squid suitable.
■ Microwave: Not suitable.

BAKED LAMB CUTLETS IN HONEY SESAME MARINADE

12 lamb cutlets

HONEY SESAME MARINADE
¼ cup light soy sauce
1 clove garlic, minced
2 tablespoons dry sherry
3 tablespoons honey
¼ teaspoon five-spice powder
1 teaspoon Oriental sesame oil
1 teaspoon sesame seeds

Scrape cutlets down the bone to meaty section, trim away excess fat. Place cutlets in shallow dish, add marinade, turn to coat completely; cover, refrigerate several hours or overnight.

Just before serving, place cutlets on wire rack over roasting pan, bake in 350°F oven about 35 minutes or until cutlets are cooked. Brush with marinade during cooking.

Honey Sesame Marinade: Combine all ingredients in bowl.

Makes 12.

■ Cutlets can be prepared 2 days ahead.
■ Storage: Covered, in refrigerator.
■ Freeze: Uncooked cutlets suitable.
■ Microwave: Not suitable.

BEEF, ASPARAGUS AND PEPPER ROLLS

14oz piece rump steak
1 tablespoon Worcestershire sauce
2 teaspoons seeded mustard
1 medium bunch (½lb) fresh asparagus
1 red bell pepper
3 tablespoons vegetable oil

Wrap steak in plastic wrap, freeze about 20 minutes or until partially frozen. Remove plastic, cut steak into thin slices.

ABOVE LEFT: Baked Lamb Cutlets in Honey Sesame Marinade.
RIGHT: From top: Crumbed Squid with Coconut Curry Sauce, Beef, Asparagus and Pepper Rolls.

CRISPY CRAB TRIANGLES

1/4 cup (1/2 stick) butter
3 green onions, chopped
1/4 cup all-purpose flour
1 cup milk
1 tablespoon lime juice
2 tablespoons chopped fresh parsley
2 x 51/2oz cans crab meat, drained
16 sheets phyllo pastry
3/4 cup (11/2 sticks) butter,
    melted, extra

Heat butter in pan, add onions, cook, stirring, until soft. Stir in flour, stir until bubbling. Remove from heat, gradually stir in milk, stir over heat until mixture boils and thickens. Stir in juice, parsley and crab; cool to room temperature.

Brush 2 sheets of pastry with some of the extra butter, layer together, cut crossways into 23/4 inch strips. Place a level teaspoon of crab mixture at 1 end of each strip. Fold ends over to form triangles, continue folding to end of strips, brush with butter. Place triangles on lightly greased baking sheet. Repeat with remaining pastry, butter and filling.
Just before serving, bake triangles in 350°F oven about 15 minutes or until lightly browned.

Makes about 60.

■ Triangles can be prepared a day ahead.
■ Storage: Covered, in refrigerator.
■ Freeze: Uncooked triangles suitable.
■ Microwave: Not suitable.

CHICKEN COCONUT BITES

3 cups (5oz) flaked coconut
2 boneless, skinless, chicken
    breast halves
all-purpose flour
1 egg, lightly beaten
3 tablespoons milk
oil for deep-frying
1 teaspoon celery salt
1/2 teaspoon garlic powder
1/2 teaspoon ground cumin

Blend or process coconut until roughly chopped. Cut chicken into 3/4 inch pieces. Toss chicken in flour, shake away excess flour. Dip chicken into combined egg and milk, then into coconut. Press coconut firmly onto chicken; cover, refrigerate 15 minutes.
Just before serving, deep-fry chicken in hot oil until golden brown and cooked. Drain on absorbent paper, sprinkle with combined salt, garlic powder and cumin.

Makes about 40.

■ Bites can be prepared a day ahead.
■ Storage: Covered, in refrigerator.
■ Freeze: Uncooked bites suitable.
■ Microwave: Not suitable.

CREAMY SMOKED SALMON TARTLETS

3 sheets (10in x 10in) ready rolled
    puff pastry
31/2oz smoked salmon,
    finely chopped
2 dill pickles, finely chopped
2 green onions, chopped
1/2 cup sour cream
1 tablespoon milk
2 eggs, lightly beaten
1 teaspoon chopped fresh dill
1/4 teaspoon paprika

Cut pastry into 21/2 inch rounds, place rounds into lightly greased 12-hole tart trays (4 teaspoon capacity). Sprinkle salmon, dill pickles and onions into pastry shells, pour in combined cream, milk, eggs, dill and paprika. Bake in 350°F oven about 30 minutes or until well browned and puffed. Serve hot.

Makes about 24.

■ Tartlets can be made 3 hours ahead.
■ Storage: Covered, in refrigerator.
■ Freeze: Cooked tartlets suitable.
■ Microwave: Not suitable.

LEFT: Clockwise from back: Creamy Smoked Salmon Tartlets, Chicken Coconut Bites, Crispy Crab Triangles.

CASHEW AND BASIL TARTLETS

**3 sheets (10in x 10in) ready rolled
    shortcrust pastry**
paprika

CASHEW FILLING
2 tablespoons (¼ stick) butter
1 onion, finely chopped
4oz package cream cheese
2 tablespoons (¼ stick) butter, extra
¼ cup roasted cashew nuts
3 tablespoons chopped fresh basil
1 egg yolk
¼ cup heavy cream
¼ cup grated fresh Parmesan cheese

Cut 2 inch rounds from pastry, press into lightly greased mini muffin pans (4 teaspoon capacity), prick well with fork. Bake in 375°F oven about 10 minutes or until lightly browned, remove from pan to wire rack.
Just before serving, spoon filling into piping bag fitted with ½ inch plain tube, pipe filling evenly into pastry cases. Place tartlets on baking sheet, bake in 350°F oven about 10 minutes or until filling is set. Sprinkle tartlets lightly with paprika just before serving.
Cashew Filling: Heat butter in pan, add onion, cook, stirring, until onion is soft. Blend or process remaining ingredients until smooth, stir in onion mixture.

Makes about 60.
■ Pastry cases and filling can be prepared a day ahead.
■ Storage: Filling, in refrigerator. Pastry cases in airtight container.
■ Freeze: Pastry cases suitable.
■ Microwave: Not suitable.

LAMB KABOBS
WITH AVOCADO APRICOT DIP

1lb lamb fillets
2 tablespoons lime juice
1 clove garlic, minced
1 tablespoon sugar
bay leaves
¾lb button mushrooms

AVOCADO APRICOT DIP
1 large avocado, chopped
1 teaspoon Tabasco sauce
1 tablespoon sour cream
⅓ cup chopped dried apricots

Trim excess fat from lamb, cut lamb into ¾ inch pieces. Combine lamb, juice, garlic and sugar in bowl; cover, refrigerate several hours or overnight.

Thread lamb, bay leaves and mushrooms onto 15 skewers.

Just before serving, broil kabobs until browned and tender. Serve hot with dip.

Avocado Apricot Dip: Blend or process avocado, sauce and sour cream until smooth; stir in apricots.

Makes 15.

■ Kabobs can be prepared a day ahead; dip an hour ahead.
■ Storage: Both, covered, in refrigerator.
■ Freeze: Not suitable.
■ Microwave: Not suitable.

ABOVE: From left: Cashew and Basil Tartlets, Lamb Kabobs with Avocado Apricot Dip.

QUICK SAUSAGE ROLLS

2 cups self-rising flour
2 teaspoons sugar
1 tablespoon butter
1 cup milk, approximately
20 (about 1lb) chipolata sausages
1 egg, lightly beaten

Sift flour and sugar into bowl, rub in butter, stir in enough milk to mix to a soft dough. Turn dough onto lightly floured surface, knead gently until smooth. Roll dough on lightly floured surface until ⅛ inch thick.

Cut dough into 3 inch x 3½ inch rectangles, lightly brush edges with water. Roll sausages in rectangles of dough, pinching ends to seal.

Place sausage rolls onto greased baking sheets, lightly brush with egg, cut 3 slits on top of each roll.

Just before serving, bake rolls in 350°F oven about 25 minutes or until browned. Cut sausage rolls in half before serving.

Makes about 40.

- Can be prepared several hours ahead.
- Storage: Covered, on baking sheet.
- Freeze: Cooked rolls suitable.
- Microwave: Not suitable.

WARM CORN AND CHIVE DIP

8oz jar corn relish
8oz container sour cream
few drops Tabasco sauce
3 tablespoons chopped fresh chives
½ cup grated cheddar cheese

Combine all ingredients in pan, stir over heat until heated through, do not boil. Serve with corn chips.

Makes about 2 cups.

- Dip can be prepared 1 day ahead.
- Storage: Covered, in refrigerator.
- Freeze: Not suitable.
- Microwave: Suitable.

DEEP-FRIED MARINATED CHICKEN

1¼lb chicken thighs, boned, skinned
¾ inch piece fresh gingerroot
2 teaspoons curry powder
½ teaspoon five-spice powder
½ teaspoon ground cumin
2 cloves garlic, minced
½ teaspoon sambal oelek
1 teaspoon sugar
1 teaspoon grated lime zest
¼ cup lime juice
cornstarch
oil for deep-frying

Cut chicken into ¾ inch cubes. Grate gingerroot finely, press between 2 spoons over large bowl to extract juice; discard pulp. Stir in chicken, curry powder, spices, garlic, sambal oelek, sugar, zest and juice; cover, refrigerate chicken mixture several hours or overnight.

Just before serving, drain chicken, toss in cornstarch, shake away excess cornstarch. Deep-fry chicken in hot oil until browned and cooked.

Makes about 30.

- Can be prepared a day ahead.
- Storage: Covered, in refrigerator.
- Freeze: Uncooked chicken suitable.
- Microwave: Not suitable.

LEFT: Clockwise from front: Warm Corn and Chive Dip, Quick Sausage Rolls, Deep-Fried Marinated Chicken.

SPICY LAMB IN RICE PAPER

2 (6oz) lamb fillets, thinly sliced
1 clove garlic, minced
1 teaspoon honey
1 teaspoon vegetable oil
1 tablespoon light soy sauce
pinch five-spice powder
½ teaspoon grated fresh gingerroot
25 sheets rice paper
1 egg, lightly beaten
oil for deep-frying

Combine lamb, garlic, honey, oil, sauce, five-spice powder and gingerroot in bowl; cover, refrigerate 30 minutes.

Cut rice paper in half crossways, brush a piece of rice paper with some egg. Place a piece of lamb at corner of paper, roll up and tuck ends in, press lightly to flatten. Repeat with remaining rice paper, egg and lamb.

Just before serving, deep-fry parcels in hot oil until crisp but not browned.

Makes about 50.

- ■ Can be prepared 2 hours ahead.
- ■ Storage: Covered, in refrigerator.
- ■ Freeze: Not suitable.
- ■ Microwave: Not suitable.

CREAMY TORTELLINI PICK-UPS

7oz mixed tortellini
2 tablespoons (¼ stick) butter
1 clove garlic, minced
¼ cup heavy cream
¼ cup grated fresh Parmesan cheese
3 tablespoons chopped fresh parsley

Add tortellini to large pan of boiling water, boil, uncovered, about 15 minutes or until tender; drain.

Heat butter in pan, stir in garlic, cook 1 minute. Stir in cream, cheese and parsley, cook 1 minute. Add tortellini to pan; mix until combined.

Cool tortellini 5 minutes before threading onto toothpicks. Serve warm.

Makes about 25.

- ■ Tortellini can be prepared several hours ahead.
- ■ Storage: Covered, in refrigerator.
- ■ Freeze: Not suitable.
- ■ Microwave: Suitable.

SMOKED CHEESE AND MOZZARELLA BALLS

¼ cup (½ stick) butter
3 green onions, chopped
¼ cup all-purpose flour
1 cup milk
½ cup shredded mozzarella cheese
1 cup (3oz) grated smoked cheese
2 tablespoons chopped fresh chives
½ cup all-purpose flour, extra
oil for deep-frying

Heat butter in pan, add onions, cook, stirring, until soft. Stir in flour, stir until bubbling. Remove from heat, gradually stir in milk, stir over heat until sauce boils and thickens. Combine cheeses, chives and extra flour in bowl, mix well, stir into hot sauce mixture; cool to room temperature.

Using floured hands, roll 2 level teaspoons of mixture into a ball, repeat with remaining mixture.

Just before serving, deep-fry balls in hot oil until golden brown, drain on absorbent paper. Serve hot.

Makes about 50.

- ■ Can be prepared several hours ahead.
- ■ Storage: At room temperature.
- ■ Freeze: Uncooked balls suitable.
- ■ Microwave: Not suitable.

RIGHT: Clockwise from right: Spicy Lamb in Rice Paper, Creamy Tortellini Pick-Ups, Smoked Cheese and Mozzarella Balls.

SMOKED TROUT PIKELETS

½ cup self-rising flour
¼ cup whole-wheat flour
½ teaspoon double-acting
   baking powder
1 egg, lightly beaten
⅔ cup milk
1 tablespoon butter, melted
1 tablespoon chopped fresh chives
2 teaspoons chopped fresh dill
½ cup grated gruyere cheese
3½oz sliced smoked trout
1 tablespoon (1oz) trout or
   salmon roe
fresh dill sprigs

Sift flours and baking powder into bowl, gradually add egg and milk, mix to a smooth batter. Stir in butter and herbs. Drop level teaspoons of mixture into heated greased heavy-based pan, cook until bubbles appear, turn pikelets, brown other side.

Just before serving, top each pikelet with a little cheese, broil until cheese is melted. Top with trout, roe and dill.

Makes about 50.

- Can be made several hours ahead.
- Storage: In airtight container.
- Freeze: Pikelets suitable.
- Microwave: Not suitable.

RATATOUILLE CRESCENTS

2 teaspoons olive oil
½ small onion, finely chopped
1 clove garlic, minced
½ small eggplant, finely chopped
½ zucchini, finely chopped
½ x 14½oz can tomatoes
¼ teaspoon sugar
1 tablespoon chopped fresh parsley
2 teaspoons chopped fresh basil
2 sheets (10in x 10in) ready rolled
   puff pastry
1 egg, lightly beaten
3 tablespoons grated Parmesan
   cheese

Heat oil in pan, add onion and garlic, cook, stirring, until onion is soft. Stir in eggplant and zucchini, stir until vegetables are soft. Stir in undrained crushed tomatoes and sugar, simmer, uncovered, about 20 minutes or until most of the liquid has evaporated. Stir in herbs; cool.

Cut pastry into 2 inch squares, top each square with 1 level teaspoon of eggplant mixture. Lightly brush edges of pastry with water, fold pastry in half diagonally, press edges with fork. Bend triangles to form crescents. Place crescents on lightly greased baking sheet, lightly brush with egg, sprinkle with cheese.

Just before serving, bake in 350°F oven about 15 minutes or until lightly browned.

Makes about 50.

- Can be prepared a day ahead.
- Storage: Covered, in refrigerator.
- Freeze: Uncooked crescents suitable.
- Microwave: Not suitable.

CHICKEN CHEESE PATTIES

1 tablespoon vegetable oil
1 onion, chopped
1 teaspoon curry powder
½ teaspoon grated fresh gingerroot
1lb ground chicken
2 teaspoons French mustard
3 tablespoons chopped fresh chives
1 cup (3½oz) fresh bread crumbs
packaged unseasoned bread crumbs
oil for shallow-frying
2oz Jarlsberg cheese, chopped

Heat oil in pan, add onion, curry powder and gingerroot, cook, stirring, until onion is soft. Combine onion mixture, chicken, mustard, chives and fresh bread crumbs in bowl. Roll 2 level teaspoons of mixture into a ball, toss in packaged bread crumbs, flatten slightly, place onto tooth-pick. Repeat with remaining mixture and bread crumbs; cover, refrigerate 1 hour.

Shallow-fry patties in hot oil until well browned and cooked through; drain on absorbent paper.

Just before serving, top each patty with a piece of cheese, broil until cheese is melted and lightly browned.

Makes about 45.

■ Patties can be prepared a day ahead.
■ Storage: Covered, in refrigerator.
■ Freeze: Cooked patties suitable.
■ Microwave: Not suitable.

LEFT: Clockwise from front: Smoked Trout Pikelets, Ratatouille Crescents, Chicken Cheese Patties.

59

CHEESE FONDUE WITH CRUNCHY RYE CUBES

1 tablespoon drained green
    peppercorns
2 cups dry white wine
1 clove garlic, minced
3⅓ cups (13oz) grated
    gruyere cheese
2¼ cups (½lb) grated Swiss cheese
1 cup (¼lb) grated cheddar cheese
¼ cup all-purpose flour

CRUNCHY RYE CUBES
30oz loaf unsliced black rye bread
¼ cup (½ stick) butter, melted
1 teaspoon dried rosemary, crushed

Combine peppercorns, wine and garlic in pan, bring to boil, simmer, uncovered, 2 minutes; remove from heat, stand mixture 1 hour. **Just before serving,** heat wine mixture in pan, stir in well combined cheeses and flour, stir over heat until mixture starts bubbling. Remove from heat, serve with crunchy rye cubes.

Crunchy Rye Cubes: Cut bread into ½ inch cubes. Combine butter and rosemary in bowl, add cubes, toss well. Place cubes on baking sheet, bake in 350°F oven 10 minutes or until crunchy; drain cubes on absorbent paper.

Makes about 4 cups fondue.

- Rye cubes can be made a day ahead.
- Storage: Cubes in airtight container.
- Freeze: Uncooked rye cubes suitable.
- Microwave: Not suitable.

SHRIMP AND PORK WONTONS

¼lb small cooked shelled shrimp
½lb ground pork
2 green onions, chopped
1 egg, separated
1 tablespoon dark soy sauce
½ teaspoon Oriental sesame oil
60 egg pastry sheets
oil for deep-frying

Chop shrimp, combine with pork, onions, egg yolk, sauce and sesame oil in bowl. Place 1 level teaspoon of shrimp mixture on center of each pastry sheet. Brush edges of sheets lightly with egg white, pleat edges, bring together in center, press firmly to seal.

Just before serving, deep-fry wontons in hot oil until lightly browned and cooked through. (Wontons can also be cooked in pan of boiling water for about 3 minutes or until cooked through.) Drain on absorbent paper. Serve hot.

Makes 60.

- Can be prepared 6 hours ahead.
- Storage: Covered, in refrigerator.
- Freeze: Uncooked wontons suitable.
- Microwave: Not suitable.

BELOW: From left: Cheese Fondue with Crunchy Rye Cubes, Shrimp and Pork Wontons.
RIGHT: From left: Crispy Beef Strips in Nutty Oat Crumbs, Baby Potatoes with Caraway Carrot Filling.

BABY POTATOES WITH CARAWAY CARROT FILLING

20 (1¼lb) baby new potatoes, unpeeled
2 medium (7oz) carrots, chopped
¼ cup sour cream
1 teaspoon caraway seeds
2 teaspoons chopped fresh chives
2 teaspoons lemon juice
3 tablespoons chopped fresh chives, extra

Boil, steam or microwave potatoes and carrots until tender, drain; cool. Blend or process carrots until smooth.

Cut tops from potatoes; discard tops. Carefully scoop out flesh from potatoes, mash flesh in bowl. Add quarter of the flesh to carrot; mix well. (Keep remaining potato for another use.) Stir in sour cream, seeds, chives and juice. Spoon carrot mixture into potatoes, sprinkle with extra chives, place on baking sheet.

Just before serving, heat potatoes in 350˚F oven about 10 minutes.

Makes 20.

- Can be prepared a day ahead.
- Storage: Covered, in refrigerator.
- Freeze: Not suitable.
- Microwave: Suitable.

CRISPY BEEF STRIPS IN NUTTY OAT CRUMBS

3 tablespoons dark brown sugar
⅔ cup crunchy oat-bran cereal
½ cup unsalted roasted peanuts
½ teaspoon ground coriander
½ teaspoon grated lime zest
½lb piece rump steak
all-purpose flour
1 egg, lightly beaten
oil for deep-frying
¼ cup lime juice

Blend or process sugar, cereal, nuts, coriander and zest until fine, transfer to bowl. Cut steak into thin strips, toss in flour, shake away excess flour, dip into egg, then cereal mixture.

Just before serving, deep-fry strips in hot oil until crisp. Serve hot, drizzled with lime juice.

Makes about 30.

- Strips can be prepared a day ahead.
- Storage: Covered in refrigerator.
- Freeze: Uncooked strips suitable.
- Microwave: Not suitable.

CORNMEAL AND SALMON MUFFINS

1 cup cornmeal
½ cup self-rising flour
3 tablespoons sugar
1 egg
1 cup buttermilk
2 eggs, extra
½ cup heavy cream
7oz can salmon, drained, flaked
4oz can whole-kernel corn, drained

Combine cornmeal, sifted flour and sugar in bowl. Stir in combined egg and buttermilk; mix well. Whisk extra eggs and cream in another bowl until combined, stir in salmon and corn.

Spoon 1½ level teaspoons of cornmeal mixture into 1 hole of greased mini muffin pans (4 teaspoon capacity), top with 1½ level teaspoons of salmon mixture. Repeat with remaining mixture. Bake in 375°F oven about 12 minutes or until muffins are lightly browned. Serve hot.

Makes about 55.

- Muffins can be made 3 hours ahead.
- Storage: Covered, on baking sheet.
- Freeze: Suitable.
- Microwave: Not suitable.

CHICKEN AND ASPARAGUS PASTRIES

4 sheets (10in x 10in) ready rolled
**   puff pastry**
1 cup (5oz) chopped cooked chicken
½ cup chopped cooked or drained
**   canned asparagus**
3 tablespoons sour cream
3 tablespoons chopped fresh chives
2oz cheddar cheese, finely chopped
1 egg, lightly beaten

Cut each pastry sheet into 4 strips, cut each strip crossways to give 3 rectangles. Roll each rectangle on lightly floured surface to a 3 inch x 4 inch rectangle.

Combine chicken, asparagus, sour cream, chives and cheese in bowl. Spoon a level teaspoon of mixture onto each pastry rectangle, lightly brush edges with egg, fold in long sides, fold in ends. Place pastries, seam-side-down, on greased baking sheets.

Just before serving, brush pastries with egg, bake in 375°F oven about 15 minutes or until lightly browned.

Makes 48.

- Can be prepared 3 hours ahead.
- Storage: Covered, in refrigerator.
- Freeze: Cooked pastries suitable.
- Microwave: Not suitable.

LEFT: From front: Chicken and Asparagus Pastries, Cornmeal and Salmon Muffins.

HERBED CHEESES IN GOLDEN BREAD CASES

1 loaf unsliced white bread
3oz (¾ stick) butter, melted
¼ cup grated gruyere cheese

FILLING
3 tablespoons butter
3 tablespoons all-purpose flour
1¼ cups milk
1 egg yolk
⅔ cup grated gruyere cheese
⅔ cup grated fresh Parmesan cheese
1 teaspoon chopped fresh chives
1 teaspoon chopped fresh basil
1 teaspoon chopped fresh oregano

Cut bread crossways into 1¼ inch slices, remove crusts. Cut slices into 3 strips, cut each strip crossways in half to make 1¼ inch x 2 inch rectangles, scoop centers from rectangles, leaving ¼ inch shells. Brush rim and edges of shells with butter, place on baking sheet, bake in 350°F oven about 15 minutes or until lightly browned. Spoon filling into cases, sprinkle with grated gruyere cheese.

Just before serving, heat cheese cases in 350°F oven about 10 minutes.

Filling: Heat butter in pan, stir in flour, cook until bubbling. Remove from heat, gradually stir in milk, stir over heat until mixture boils and thickens. Remove from heat, stir in egg yolk and cheeses, stir over low heat until smooth, stir in herbs.

Makes about 36.

- Bread cases can be made a day ahead; filling an hour ahead.
- Storage: Bread cases in airtight container. Filling at room temperature.
- Freeze: Not suitable.
- Microwave: Not suitable.

GINGERED LAMB TURNOVERS

1½ cups all-purpose flour
¾ cup boiling water
1 egg white, lightly beaten
oil for deep-frying

FILLING
1 tablespoon vegetable oil
1 clove garlic, minced
2 teaspoons grated fresh gingerroot
½ teaspoon ground coriander
½lb ground lamb
4 green onions, chopped
2 tablespoons dark soy sauce

Sift flour into bowl, stir in boiling water, mix to a firm dough. Knead dough gently on lightly floured surface until smooth; cover, stand 15 minutes.

Roll half the dough on lightly floured surface until ¹⁄₁₆ inch thick, cut 3 inch rounds from dough. Repeat with remaining dough. Place 1 level teaspoon of filling on each round, brush edges lightly with egg white, fold rounds in half, press edges together to seal.

Just before serving, deep-fry turnovers in hot oil until well browned and heated

through; drain on absorbent paper.

Filling: Heat oil in pan, add garlic, gingerroot and coriander, cook 1 minute. Add lamb, cook, stirring about 5 minutes or until well browned. Stir in onions and sauce; cool.

Makes about 36.

- Can be prepared a day ahead.
- Storage: Covered in refrigerator.
- Freeze: Uncooked turnovers suitable.
- Microwave: Not suitable.

PORK AND VEAL ROLLS IN CRISP NOODLE CRUMBS

10oz ground pork and veal
2 cloves garlic, minced
1 teaspoon grated fresh gingerroot
½ teaspoon ground cumin
½ teaspoon ground coriander
1 small fresh red chili
**   pepper, chopped**
2 green onions, chopped
¼ cup canned drained water
**   chestnuts, chopped**
1 egg white, lightly beaten
2 teaspoons cornstarch
2 teaspoons light soy sauce
¼ teaspoon Oriental sesame oil
½lb fresh egg noodles, chopped
oil for deep-frying

Combine all ingredients except noodles and oil for deep-frying in bowl. Roll 2 level teaspoons of mixture into a log shape, roll in noodles. Repeat with remaining mixture and noodles.

Just before serving, deep-fry rolls in hot oil until well browned and cooked through; drain on absorbent paper.

Makes about 25.

- Rolls can be prepared 2 days ahead.
- Storage: Covered, in refrigerator.
- Freeze: Uncooked rolls suitable.
- Microwave: Not suitable.

RIGHT: Clockwise from left: Herbed Cheeses in Golden Bread Cases, Gingered Lamb Turnovers, Pork and Veal Rolls in Crisp Noodle Crumbs.

Cold Savories

Some of these tempting appetizers are cooked, some are uncooked, and all are served cold. Some can be made entirely in advance; others are completed just before serving. They make an easy start to your party and, while they are being served, you have the chance to cook (or finish) the hot savories you've planned. When preparing or making ahead, keep food well covered with plastic wrap in the refrigerator or airtight container, as indicated in recipes; it is important to exclude as much air as possible. Some of these savories benefit from being served at room temperature; see recipes.

EGG AND TOMATO PICKS WITH GARLIC MAYONNAISE

24 quail eggs
½lb small cherry tomatoes, halved
1 bunch fresh basil

GARLIC MAYONNAISE
1 egg
1 egg yolk
1 tablespoon lemon juice
1 cup vegetable oil
1 tablespoon chopped fresh chives
1 clove garlic, minced

Place quail eggs in pan, cover with cold water, bring to boil, simmer, uncovered, 3 minutes. Drain eggs, rinse under cold water; cool, remove shells.

Cut eggs in half, thread eggs, tomatoes and basil leaves onto toothpicks. Serve with garlic mayonnaise.

Garlic Mayonnaise: Blend or process egg, egg yolk and juice until smooth. With motor operating, gradually add oil in thin stream, blend until thickened. Stir in chives and garlic.

Makes 48.

■ Can be made 3 hours ahead.
■ Storage: Covered, in refrigerator.
■ Freeze: Not suitable.
■ Microwave: Not suitable.

MEATBALLS IN CHEESY PASTRY

1 cup all-purpose flour
pinch cayenne pepper
3oz (¾ stick) butter
1 ¼ cups (5oz) grated
   cheddar cheese
1 egg, lightly beaten
3 tablespoons sesame seeds

MEATBALLS
½lb ground beef
1 teaspoon grated lime zest
1 tablespoon lime juice

Process flour, pepper and butter until combined. Add cheese, process until mixture forms a ball. Knead dough on lightly floured surface until smooth; cover, refrigerate 30 minutes.

Roll pastry between sheets of baking paper until ¹⁄₁₆ inch thick. Cut 1¾ inch rounds from pastry, top each round with a meatball. Fold pastry around to enclose meatballs. Brush tops with egg, sprinkle with seeds, place about 1¼ inches apart on greased baking sheets. Cover, refrigerate 30 minutes.

Bake pastry-covered meatballs in 375°F oven about 15 minutes or until lightly browned; cool before serving.

Meatballs: Combine all ingredients in bowl; mix well. Roll level teaspoons of mixture into balls.

Makes about 45.

■ Can be made 3 hours ahead.
■ Storage: Covered, in refrigerator.
■ Freeze: Cooked meatballs suitable.
■ Microwave: Not suitable.

SMOKED TROUT WITH CREME FRAICHE

1 medium (3½oz) potato,
   finely chopped
3 tablespoons mayonnaise
7oz sliced smoked trout
1 bunch (about 20) chives

CREME FRAICHE
½ cup whipping cream
½ cup sour cream

Boil, steam or microwave potato until tender, drain. Combine potato and mayonnaise in bowl while still hot; cool.

Spoon potato mixture onto trout slices, fold in sides and roll up to form parcels.

Drop chives in pan of boiling water; drain immediately. Tie each parcel with a chive, trim chive ends; serve parcels with creme fraiche.

Creme Fraiche: Combine creams in bowl, cover, leave at room temperature until thick; this will take 1 or 2 days, depending on weather. Refrigerate creme fraiche until required.

Makes about 20.

■ Parcels can be made 6 hours ahead; creme fraiche a week ahead.
■ Storage: Both, covered, in refrigerator.
■ Freeze: Not suitable.
■ Microwave: Potato suitable.

RIGHT: From back: Egg and Tomato Picks with Garlic Mayonnaise, Meatballs in Cheesy Pastry, Smoked Trout with Creme Fraiche.

CREAMY SHRIMP
IN NOODLE NESTS

1 slice bacon, chopped
3 tablespoons sour cream
3½oz fresh egg noodles
3 tablespoons vegetable oil
24 small cooked shrimp, shelled
1 tablespoon alfalfa sprouts

Cook bacon in pan until crisp; cool. Combine bacon with sour cream.

Place egg noodles in bowl, cover with hot water, stand 5 minutes; drain well. Divide noodles evenly between 24 oiled mini muffin pans (4 teaspoon capacity), press firmly into pans, brush lightly and evenly with oil. Bake in 350°F oven about 15 minutes or until crisp.

Remove nests from pans with metal spatula, place upside down on wire rack, place rack on baking sheet, return to oven for about 5 minutes or until nests are crisp; cool to room temperature.
Just before serving, top each nest with a shrimp, sour cream mixture and sprouts.
Makes 24.

■ Nests can be made 3 days ahead.
■ Storage: In airtight container.
■ Freeze: Nests suitable.
■ Microwave: Not suitable.

SPICY SOUR CREAM SCONES

1¼ cups self-rising flour
¼ teaspoon turmeric
½ teaspoon curry powder
2 tablespoons (¼ stick) butter
¼ teaspoon fennel seeds
1 green onion, chopped
½ cup sour cream
¼ cup milk, approximately
8oz container sour cream, extra
fresh fennel sprigs

Sift dry ingredients into bowl, rub in butter, stir in seeds, onion, sour cream and enough milk to mix to a firm dough. Knead dough on lightly floured surface until smooth, roll dough until ½ inch thick. Cut into 1½ inch rounds, place on greased baking sheet. Bake in 400°F oven about 12 minutes or until scones are lightly browned and sound hollow when tapped on bases; cool on wire rack.
Just before serving, break scones in half, sandwich with extra sour cream and fennel sprigs.
Makes about 45.

■ Scones can be made 3 hours ahead.
■ Storage: In airtight container.
■ Freeze: Unfilled scones suitable.
■ Microwave: Not suitable.

BARBEQUED PORK
ON RICE CRACKERS

30 plain rice crackers
7oz piece Chinese barbequed
    pork, sliced
1 tablespoon hoisin sauce
½ teaspoon water
3 tablespoons canned drained water
    chestnuts, chopped
2 green onions, chopped

Top each rice cracker with pork. Place combined sauce and water into small piping bag fitted with small plain tube, pipe thin lines over pork. Top with water chestnuts and onions.

Makes 30.

■ Can be made 30 minutes ahead.
■ Storage: Covered, in refrigerator.
■ Freeze: Not suitable.

LEFT: Creamy Shrimp in Noodle Nests.
ABOVE: From left: Spicy Sour Cream Scones, Barbequed Pork on Rice Crackers.

SMOKED TROUT
AND AVOCADO FINGERS

½ (¼lb) smoked trout,
skinned, boned
½ large avocado, chopped
1 tablespoon lemon juice
2 tablespoons sour cream
¼ teaspoon lemon pepper
¼ teaspoon horseradish cream
8 slices white bread
¼ cup (½ stick) butter, softened

Blend or process trout, avocado, juice, cream, pepper and horseradish until smooth; cover, refrigerate several hours.

Remove and discard crusts from bread, butter each side of bread, cut each slice in half, then each half into 4 fingers. Place bread on baking sheet, bake in 350°F oven for 6 minutes, turn bread over, bake further 6 minutes or until lightly browned; cool. Spoon trout mixture into piping bag fitted with small fluted tube, pipe mixture onto toast fingers.

Makes 64.

■ Fingers can be made 4 hours ahead.
■ Storage: Covered, in refrigerator.
■ Freeze: Toast fingers suitable.
■ Microwave: Not suitable.

CURRIED PEPITAS
AND MACADAMIAS

3 tablespoons vegetable oil
1 tablespoon curry powder
½ teaspoon rock salt
¾ cup pepitas
1¼ cups (6oz) macadamias

Combine oil and curry powder in roasting pan, stir over heat for about 2 minutes, or until fragrant. Add salt, pepitas and nuts, stir until coated with oil. Bake in 350°F oven for about 10 minutes or until lightly browned, stirring occasionally; cool.

Makes about 2 cups.

■ Recipe can be made 3 weeks ahead.
■ Storage: In airtight container.
■ Freeze: Suitable.
■ Microwave: Not suitable.

GREEN OLIVES IN HERB
AND ONION MARINADE

1lb green olives, pitted
1 small onion, finely chopped
1 stalk celery, finely chopped
¼ cup olive oil
¼ cup white vinegar
pinch chili powder
2 tablespoons chopped fresh basil
2 teaspoons chopped fresh oregano
2 teaspoons chopped fresh chives

Combine all ingredients in bowl; refrigerate overnight.

Makes about 2 cups.

■ Olives can be made a month ahead.
■ Storage: Covered, in refrigerator.
■ Freeze: Not suitable.

ORANGE AND SMOKED
TURKEY CUBES

4oz package cream cheese
pinch paprika
9 slices white bread
5oz sliced smoked turkey
½ avocado, mashed
1 orange, segmented

Beat cheese and paprika in bowl with electric mixer until smooth. Spread 3 bread slices with some cheese mixture, top with a layer of turkey, then spread thinly with avocado. Spread another 3 slices of bread with cheese mixture, place cheese-side-down on previous slices. Repeat spreading and layering with remaining cheese mixture, turkey, avocado and bread. Cut crusts from sandwiches, cut sandwiches into 3 fingers, cut fingers into 3 cubes. Toothpick a small piece of orange onto each cube.

Makes 27.

■ Cubes can be made 2 hours ahead.
■ Storage: Covered, in refrigerator.
■ Freeze: Not suitable.

ABOVE: Orange and Smoked Turkey Cubes. RIGHT: Clockwise from top: Curried Pepitas and Macadamias, Smoked Trout and Avocado Fingers, Green Olives in Herb and Onion Marinade.

PASTRAMI HORSERADISH CONES

1 sheet (10in x 10in) ready rolled puff pastry
1 egg white, lightly beaten

PASTRAMI HORSERADISH FILLING
1 egg yolk
1 teaspoon white vinegar
1 tablespoon horseradish cream
½ cup vegetable oil
6 slices pastrami, chopped
2 dill pickles, chopped

Lightly grease small cream horn molds.

Cut pastry into ½ inch strips, cut each strip in half crossways. Brush each strip lightly with egg white. Starting at point of each mold, wind pastry strips, egg white side out, around molds, overlapping edges of pastry slightly.

Place cones on lightly greased baking sheet, seam-side-down, brush lightly with egg white. Bake in 400˚F oven 5 minutes, reduce heat to 350˚F, bake further 8 minutes or until cones are browned and crisp. Remove cones from molds, cool on wire rack. Repeat with remaining pastry and egg white.

Just before serving, fill cones with filling.
Pastrami Horseradish Filling: Blend or process egg yolk, vinegar and horseradish cream until smooth. Add oil gradually in thin stream while motor is operating, blend until thickened. Stir in pastrami and dill pickles, refrigerate 1 hour.

Makes about 50.

■ Cones and filling can be made separately 2 days ahead.
■ Storage: Cones, in airtight container. Filling, covered, in refrigerator.
■ Freeze: Unfilled cones suitable.
■ Microwave: Not suitable.

POPPYSEED CRACKERS WITH TWO DIPS

1 cup self-rising flour
¾ cup all-purpose flour
2 teaspoons poppy seeds
2 teaspoons dried oregano leaves
1 teaspoon ground black peppercorns
½ teaspoon chili powder
3 tablespoons tomato paste
2 tablespoons vegetable oil
½ cup water

TOMATO DIP
1 tomato, finely chopped
2 green onions, chopped
1 small onion, finely chopped
2 tablespoons chopped fresh mint
1 tablespoon white vinegar

SOUR CREAM DIP
8oz container sour cream
1 tablespoon lemon juice
1 tablespoon chopped fresh dill

Sift flours into bowl, stir in seeds, oregano, pepper and chili, then combined paste, oil and water, mix to a firm dough. Knead dough on lightly floured surface; cover, refrigerate 30 minutes.

Roll out dough on lightly floured surface until ⅛ inch thick. Cut 2¼ inch rounds from dough. Place on greased baking sheets, bake in 350˚F oven for about 15 minutes or until lightly browned; cool on wire racks. Serve crackers with dips.
Tomato Dip: Squeeze excess moisture from tomato, combine in bowl with remaining ingredients.
Sour Cream Dip: Combine all ingredients in bowl; mix well.

Makes about 80 crackers.

■ Crackers can be made a week ahead. Dips can be made a day ahead.
■ Storage: Crackers, in airtight container. Dips, covered, in refrigerator.
■ Freeze: Not suitable.
■ Microwave: Not suitable.

LEFT: Pastrami Horseradish Cones.
ABOVE: Poppyseed Crackers with Two Dips.

PESTO DIP WITH CRISP GARLIC WEDGES

1 cup chopped fresh basil
1 clove garlic, minced
3 tablespoons pine nuts, toasted
3 tablespoons grated fresh
   Parmesan cheese
3 tablespoons olive oil
2 teaspoons lemon juice
8oz container sour cream

CRISP GARLIC WEDGES
4 rounds pita bread
5oz (1¼ sticks) butter, melted
2 cloves garlic, minced
⅔ cup grated fresh Parmesan cheese

Blend or process basil, garlic, nuts, cheese, oil and juice until smooth. Combine in bowl with sour cream; serve with crisp garlic wedges.

Crisp Garlic Wedges: Split bread rounds in half, cut into large wedges, place split-side-up on baking sheets. Brush with combined butter and garlic, sprinkle with cheese. Bake in 375°F oven for about 8 minutes or until lightly browned and crisp.

■ Both can be made a day ahead.
■ Storage: Dip, covered, in refrigerator. Wedges, in airtight container.
■ Freeze: Wedges suitable.
■ Microwave: Not suitable.

CHEESY HAM AND CANTALOUPE BALLS

11oz can leg ham, chopped
8oz package cream cheese, chopped
1 tablespoon orange marmalade
2 teaspoons ground gingerroot
¾ cup sesame seeds, toasted
1 cantaloupe

Process ham until finely chopped, add cheese, marmalade and gingerroot, process until smooth. Transfer mixture to bowl; cover, refrigerate 1 hour or until firm.

Shape 1½ level teaspoons of mixture into balls, toss in seeds, place on tray, refrigerate until firm. Using a melon baller, scoop balls from cantaloupe.

Just before serving, thread cheesy ham balls and cantaloupe balls onto toothpicks.

Makes about 50.
- Recipe can be prepared a day ahead.
- Storage: Covered, in refrigerator.
- Freeze: Not suitable.

BEEF CROUTES
WITH MUSTARD MAYONNAISE

1lb piece beef tenderloin
3 tablespoons vegetable oil
2 small French bread sticks
1 tablespoon butter, melted
1 tablespoon vegetable oil, extra
fresh tarragon

MUSTARD MAYONNAISE
½ cup mayonnaise
1 tablespoon seeded mustard
2 tablespoons chopped fresh tarragon

Secure beef with kitchen string at 1¼ inch intervals. Heat oil in roasting pan, add beef, cook until well browned all over. Bake in pan in hot oven for about 15 minutes or until beef is done as desired; cool.

Cut bread into ½ inch slices, brush with combined butter and extra oil, place on baking sheet. Bake in 350°F oven about 5 minutes or until lightly browned and crisp; cool. Cut beef into thin slices.

Just before serving, top bread with beef, mayonnaise and tarragon.

Mustard Mayonnaise: Combine all ingredients in bowl.

Makes about 40.

- Beef, bread and mayonnaise can be prepared separately a day ahead.
- Storage: Beef and mayonnaise, covered, in refrigerator. Bread, in airtight container.
- Freeze: Bread suitable.
- Microwave: Not suitable.

LEFT: Pesto Dip with Crisp Garlic Wedges.
ABOVE: From left: Beef Croutes with Mustard Mayonnaise, Cheesy Ham and Cantaloupe Balls.

NUTTY NIBBLE MIX

**2½ cups (3½oz) chunky
  breakfast cereal**
7oz package soya crisps
⅓ cup unroasted unsalted peanuts
**⅓ cup unroasted unsalted
  cashews**
⅓ cup almond kernels
⅓ cup unsalted macadamias
⅔ cup pepitas
¼ cup olive oil
½ cup (1 stick) butter
1 tablespoon ground cumin
1 teaspoon ground coriander
¼ teaspoon ground cardamom
1½ teaspoons garam masala
½ teaspoon garlic powder
2 teaspoons celery salt
½ teaspoon ground black pepper

Combine cereal, crisps, nuts and pepitas in large bowl. Heat oil and butter in pan, stir in spices, salt and pepper, stir until foaming, pour over cereal mixture; mix well. Spread mixture on 2 baking sheets in single layer, bake in 325˚F oven for about 35 minutes or until mix has dried out. Cool on baking sheets.

Makes about 4½ cups.

■ Mix can be made 1 month ahead.
■ Storage: In airtight container.
■ Freeze: Not suitable.
■ Microwave: Not suitable.

*ABOVE: From front: Smoked Turkey and
Cranberry Rounds, Nutty Nibble Mix.
RIGHT: From front: Cucumber Rounds with
Herbed Cream Cheese, Roast Beef and
Avocado on Pumpernickel.*

SMOKED TURKEY AND CRANBERRY ROUNDS

3 large cabbage leaves
10oz ricotta cheese
10oz sliced smoked turkey breast
⅓ cup cranberry sauce
watercress sprigs

Spread leaves with cheese, top with turkey slices. Cut into 1½ inch rounds.
Just before serving, top rounds with sauce and watercress.

Makes about 65.

■ Rounds can be prepared a day ahead.
■ Storage: Covered, in refrigerator.
■ Freeze: Not suitable.

CUCUMBER ROUNDS WITH HERBED CREAM CHEESE

4oz package cream cheese
1 tablespoon sour cream
1 tablespoon chopped fresh basil
2 tablespoons chopped fresh parsley
1 teaspoon chopped fresh oregano
1/4 teaspoon chopped fresh rosemary
2 green onions, chopped
1 teaspoon lemon juice
1 long green cucumber
fresh oregano sprigs, extra

Blend or process cheese, cream, herbs, onions and juice until smooth. Cut cucumber into 1/4 inch slices, top with cheese mixture, then extra oregano and pieces of red bell pepper, if desired. Cover, refrigerate for 2 hours.

Makes about 20.

■ Rounds can be made 3 hours ahead.
■ Storage: Covered, in refrigerator.
■ Freeze: Not suitable.

ROAST BEEF AND AVOCADO ON PUMPERNICKEL

3½oz packaged cream cheese
1/4 avocado, mashed
1 teaspoon lemon juice
1/4 small red bell pepper, finely chopped
6oz sliced roast beef
½ cup (1 stick) butter
2 tablespoons chopped fresh parsley
½lb sliced pumpernickel rounds
fresh parsley sprigs, extra

Beat cheese, avocado and half the juice in bowl with electric mixer until well combined; stir in pepper. Spread cheese mixture over beef slices, roll slices tightly; cover, refrigerate until firm. Cut beef rolls into 1/4 inch slices diagonally.

Beat butter, parsley and remaining juice in bowl until smooth. Spoon mixture into piping bag fitted with fluted tube. Pipe swirls of butter mixture onto pumpernickel rounds, top with beef roll slices and extra parsley sprigs.

Makes about 24.

■ Rolls can be made 3 hours ahead.
■ Storage: Covered, in refrigerator.
■ Freeze: Not suitable.

OYSTERS WITH RED BELL PEPPER DRESSING

40 oysters in shells
1 red bell pepper
½ cup vegetable oil
3 tablespoons lemon juice
1 teaspoon grated fresh gingerroot
1 tablespoon chopped fresh dill
2 teaspoons sour cream
fresh dill sprigs, extra

Remove oysters from shells, wash and dry shells; drain oysters on absorbent paper. Quarter pepper, remove seeds and membrane. Broil pepper, skin-side-up, until skin blisters. Peel skin, chop three-quarters of the pepper. Cut remaining pepper into thin strips; reserve strips. Blend or process chopped pepper, oil, juice, gingerroot, dill and sour cream until smooth. Combine mixture with oysters in bowl; cover, refrigerate 2 hours.

Just before serving, return oysters to shells, top with a little of the dressing, extra dill and reserved pepper.

Makes 40.

- Oysters and dressing can be prepared a day ahead.
- Storage: Covered, in refrigerator.
- Freeze: Not suitable.
- Microwave: Not suitable.

EGG AND HORSERADISH PUFFS

3oz (¾ stick) butter
1 cup water
1 cup all-purpose flour
4 eggs, lightly beaten
FILLING
5oz ricotta cheese
5 hard-boiled eggs
1½ teaspoons horseradish cream
½ teaspoon paprika
¼ teaspoon lemon juice

Combine butter and water in pan, bring to boil, stirring, until butter is melted. Add sifted flour all at once, stir vigorously over heat until mixture leaves side of pan and forms a smooth ball. Place mixture in bowl of electric mixer or processor. Add eggs gradually, beating well after each addition.

Spoon mixture into piping bag fitted with star tube, pipe 2 inch lengths about ¾ inch apart onto lightly greased baking sheets. Bake in 350°F oven about 20 minutes or until puffs are lightly browned and crisp; cool.

Just before serving, cut puffs in half, pipe or spoon filling into centers.

Filling: Blend or process all ingredients until smooth.

Makes about 35.

- Puffs and filling can be made a day ahead separately.
- Storage: Puffs, in airtight container. Filling, covered, in refrigerator.
- Freeze: Unfilled puffs suitable.
- Microwave: Not suitable.

THYME CRISPS

We had best results using a mortar and pestle, but thyme and salt can be crushed and chopped together.

10 x 4in square egg pastry sheets
2 teaspoons chopped fresh thyme
1 teaspoon coarse (Kosher) salt
oil for deep-frying

Cut pastry sheets in half, cut halves crossways into ¾ inch strips. Grind thyme and salt together using mortar and pestle. Deep-fry pastry strips in hot oil about 5 seconds or until lightly browned; drain on absorbent paper. Sprinkle with thyme mixture; cool before serving.

Makes about 100.

- Crisps can be made 2 weeks ahead.
- Storage: In airtight container.
- Freeze: Not suitable.
- Microwave: Not suitable.

LEFT: Clockwise from front: Thyme Crisps, Egg and Horseradish Puffs, Oysters with Red Bell Pepper Dressing.

BLUE CHEESE APRICOT SWIRLS

3½oz blue vein cheese
3½oz packaged cream cheese
½ teaspoon drained green
   peppercorns, crushed
2 teaspoons chopped fresh basil
24 (¼lb) dried apricot halves
6 pitted black olives

Beat cheeses in bowl with electric mixer until smooth, beat in peppercorns and basil. Spoon mixture into piping bag fitted with fluted tube, pipe swirls of mixture onto apricots. Cut olives into slivers, top each swirl with 2 olive slivers.

Makes 24.

■ Recipe can be made 3 hours ahead.
■ Storage: Covered, in refrigerator.
■ Freeze: Not suitable.

CHICKEN PEARL BALLS WITH MANGO SAUCE

¾lb ground chicken
1 tablespoon hoisin sauce
1 tablespoon light soy sauce
¼ teaspoon five-spice powder
½ teaspoon Oriental sesame oil
½ cup fresh bread crumbs
1½ cups uncooked long-grain rice
MANGO SAUCE
1 mango, chopped
3 tablespoons plain yogurt
1 tablespoon water
pinch five-spice powder

Combine chicken, sauces, spice powder, oil and bread crumbs in bowl. Toss 2 level teaspoons of mixture into rice, shape into a ball. Repeat with remaining mixture and rice. Place balls in single layer in top half of steamer, cook, covered, over simmering water about 40 minutes or until rice is tender; cool before serving with sauce.
Sauce: Blend or process mango, yogurt, water and spice powder until smooth.

Makes about 30.

■ Chicken balls and sauce can be made a day ahead.
■ Storage: Covered, in refrigerator.
■ Freeze: Chicken balls suitable.
■ Microwave: Not suitable.

LEEK AND MUSTARD PIES

3 cups all-purpose flour
5oz (1¼ sticks) butter
1 egg
⅔ cup water, approximately
1 egg, lightly beaten, extra
FILLING
1 large (13oz) leek, roughly chopped
1 carrot, roughly chopped
3oz (¾ stick) butter
¼ cup heavy cream
1 tablespoon seeded mustard

Sift flour into bowl, rub in butter, add egg and enough water to mix to a firm dough. Knead dough on floured surface until smooth; cover, refrigerate 30 minutes.

Roll half the pastry on lightly floured surface until ¼ inch thick, cut into 3½ inch rounds. Place rounds into greased deep 12-hole cup cake trays (3 tablespoon capacity), spoon in filling, lightly brush pastry edges with extra egg.

Roll out remaining pastry, cut 3 inch rounds from pastry, cut a small hole in center of each round. Place rounds over filling, press edges of pastry to seal; brush tops with more extra egg. Bake pies in 350°F oven about 35 minutes or until well browned; cool on wire racks.
Just before serving, cut pies into quarters, serve at room temperature.
Filling: Process leek until finely chopped. Process carrot separately until finely chopped. Heat butter in pan, add leek and carrot, cook, stirring, until carrot is soft. Stir in cream and mustard, cook, uncovered, about 10 minutes or until thick; cool.

Makes 60.

■ Pies can be made a day ahead.
■ Storage: Covered, in refrigerator.
■ Freeze: Not suitable.
■ Microwave: Not suitable.

RIGHT: Clockwise from right: Leek and Mustard Pies, Blue Cheese Apricot Swirls, Chicken Pearl Balls with Mango Sauce.

CHICKEN AND ALMOND RIBBON SANDWICHES

**7oz packaged cream
   cheese, softened
½ teaspoon ground gingerroot
½ teaspoon five-spice powder
¾ cup (1½ sticks) butter
¼ cup chopped fresh parsley
10 slices whole-wheat bread
5 slices white bread
5 slices premium chicken loaf
⅓ cup sliced almonds, toasted**

Beat cheese and spices in small bowl with electric mixer until smooth. Beat butter and parsley in bowl until smooth.

Spread 5 slices of whole-wheat bread with cheese mixture, top with white bread slices. Spread with half the butter mixture, top with chicken, sprinkle with almonds. Spread remaining whole-wheat bread with remaining butter mixture, place butter-side-down, on chicken. Cut crusts from sandwiches, cut sandwiches into thirds, cut each third into 3 pieces.

Makes 45.

■ Sandwiches can be made several hours ahead.
■ Storage: Covered, in refrigerator.
■ Freeze: Suitable.

PUMPKIN SQUASH RICOTTA BALLS

**7oz pumpkin squash, chopped
4 green onions, chopped
4oz package cream cheese
¼lb ricotta cheese
½ teaspoon ground nutmeg
1 teaspoon chopped fresh dill
1½ cups (5oz) packaged unseasoned
   bread crumbs
1 egg, lightly beaten
½ cup cornmeal
oil for deep-frying**

Boil, steam or microwave squash until soft; drain. Mash squash in bowl; cool. Blend or process squash, onions, cheeses, nutmeg, dill and bread crumbs until mixture forms a smooth ball. Roll 2 level teaspoons of mixture into a ball, dip in egg, then toss in cornmeal. Repeat with remaining mixture, egg and cornmeal. Deep-fry in hot oil until browned, drain on absorbent paper; cool before serving.

Makes about 50.

■ Balls can be made 2 days ahead.
■ Storage: Covered, in refrigerator.
■ Freeze: Not suitable.
■ Microwave: Not suitable.

DUCK AND GINGER TARTLETS

**1 tablespoon vegetable oil
5oz boneless, skinless duck
   breast half
¼ cup redcurrant jelly, melted
¼ cup fresh parsley sprigs**

PASTRY
**1 cup all-purpose flour
¼ cup (½ stick) butter
1 egg yolk
1 tablespoon lemon juice
1 tablespoon water, approximately**

FILLING
**1 large onion, chopped
1½ teaspoons grated fresh gingerroot
⅓ cup water
3 tablespoons marmalade**

Heat oil in pan, add duck, cook until browned all over and tender; cool. Cut duck into thin strips.

Roll pastry on lightly floured surface until ¼ inch thick. Cut 2¾ inch rounds from pastry, place into greased 12-hole tart tray, prick all over with fork. Bake in 350°F oven about 15 minutes or until pastry is lightly browned; cool.

Spoon filling into pastry cases, top with duck, brush with jelly, top with parsley; cover, refrigerate 1 hour before serving.

Pastry: Sift flour into bowl, rub in butter. Add egg yolk, juice and enough water to mix to a firm dough. Knead dough on lightly floured surface until smooth; cover, refrigerate 30 minutes.

Filling: Combine onion, gingerroot and water in pan. Bring to boil, simmer, covered, about 15 minutes or until onion is very soft. Blend or process onion mixture and marmalade until smooth; cool.

Makes 12.

■ Tartlets can be made 3 hours ahead.
■ Storage: Covered, in refrigerator.
■ Freeze: Not suitable.
■ Microwave: Not suitable.

ABOVE LEFT: From left: Chicken and Almond Ribbon Sandwiches, Pumpkin Squash Ricotta Balls.
ABOVE: Duck and Ginger Tartlets.

ROAST BEEF AND DILL PICKLE TARTLETS

1½ sheets (10 in x 10 in) ready rolled shortcrust pastry
3½oz sliced roast beef, finely shredded
4 small dill pickles, finely chopped
1 tablespoon chopped fresh parsley
3 tablespoons chopped fresh chives
3 tablespoons tomato paste
¼ cup mayonnaise
¼ cup fresh parsley sprigs, extra

Cut 1½ inch squares from pastry, press into greased 1½ inch tart pans, prick all over with fork. Bake in 350°F oven about 10 minutes or until lightly browned; cool.

Combine beef, dill pickles, herbs, paste and mayonnaise in bowl.

Just before serving, fill pastry cases with beef mixture, top with extra parsley.

Makes about 30.

■ Tartlets can be made 2 hours ahead.
■ Storage: Covered, in refrigerator.
■ Freeze: Unfilled pastry cases suitable.
■ Microwave: Not suitable.

CHICKEN AND CILANTRO TOASTS

15 slices white bread
¾lb chicken thighs, boned, skinned, chopped
1 egg
2 teaspoons dry sherry
2 teaspoons light soy sauce
2 teaspoons cornstarch
½ teaspoon grated fresh gingerroot
1 tablespoon canned unsweetened coconut cream
1 egg, lightly beaten, extra
¼ cup fresh cilantro sprigs
oil for deep-frying

Cut a 3 inch square from each bread slice, cut each square into 4 triangles. Blend or process chicken, egg, sherry, sauce, cornstarch, gingerroot and coconut cream until smooth. Spread each triangle with chicken mixture, brush lightly with extra egg, top with a cilantro sprig.

Up to 1 hour before serving, deep-fry triangles in hot oil until well browned; drain on absorbent paper; cool.

Makes 60.

■ Toasts can be prepared 1 day ahead.
■ Storage: Covered, in refrigerator.
■ Freeze: Uncooked toasts suitable.
■ Microwave: Not suitable.

AVOCADO ANCHOVY DIP

1 avocado, mashed
2oz can anchovy fillets, drained, finely chopped
1 clove garlic, finely chopped
¼ red bell pepper, finely chopped
1 small onion, finely chopped
3 tablespoons sour cream
1 teaspoon lemon juice

Combine all ingredients in bowl; cover, refrigerate 1 hour. Serve with crackers.

Makes about 1 cup.

■ Dip can be made 3 hours ahead.
■ Storage: Covered, in refrigerator.
■ Freeze: Not suitable.

ABOVE: Clockwise from front: Roast Beef and Dill Pickle Tartlets, Avocado Anchovy Dip, Chicken and Cilantro Toasts.
RIGHT: Clockwise from left: Roast Beef and Cucumber Mini Sandwiches, Omelet Rolls with Trout and Pepper Cheese, Pumpernickel Cheese Truffles.

OMELET ROLLS WITH TROUT AND PEPPER CHEESE

7oz green peppercorn cheese
4 eggs
7oz smoked trout, chopped
1 small avocado, mashed
2 teaspoons lemon juice

Freeze cheese until firm enough to grate.

Beat eggs in bowl until combined. Pour quarter of egg mixture into heated well-greased heavy-based crepe pan, cook until set, lift onto plate; cover. Repeat with remaining eggs.

Place quarter of trout along a side of 1 omelet, top with some of the combined avocado and juice, then grated cheese. Repeat with remaining omelets, trout, avocado mixture and cheese. Carefully roll omelets, wrap in plastic wrap, refrigerate for 2 hours.

Just before serving, cut each roll into ¾ inch slices.

Makes about 24.

■ Rolls can be prepared a day ahead.
■ Storage: Covered, in refrigerator.
■ Freeze: Not suitable.
■ Microwave: Not suitable.

PUMPERNICKEL CHEESE TRUFFLES

3oz (¾ stick) butter
¾ cup finely grated Edam cheese
½ teaspoon paprika
pinch cayenne pepper
dash Tabasco sauce
¼lb pumpernickel bread

Beat butter, cheese, spices and sauce in small bowl with electric mixer until smooth and creamy; cover, refrigerate mixture for 30 minutes.

Blend or process pumpernickel until coarsely crumbed. Roll level teaspoons of cheese mixture in pumpernickel crumbs; cover, refrigerate 30 minutes or until firm.

Makes about 30.

■ Truffles can be made 3 days ahead.
■ Storage: Covered, in refrigerator.
■ Freeze: Suitable.

ROAST BEEF AND CUCUMBER MINI SANDWICHES

2oz packaged cream cheese
2 tablespoons chopped fresh chives
3 tablespoons butter
1 teaspoon seeded mustard
3 slices whole-wheat bread
1 small green cucumber, thinly sliced
3 slices light grain bread
3½oz sliced rare roast beef
3 slices white bread

Beat cheese and chives in bowl. Beat butter and mustard in separate bowl until smooth. Spread cheese mixture over whole-wheat bread slices, top with cucumber. Spread butter mixture over grain bread slices, top with beef.

Stack grain bread slices on whole-wheat bread slices; top with white bread slices. Cut off crusts, cut each sandwich in half then each half into 4 fingers.

Makes 24.

■ Can be made 1 hour ahead.
■ Storage: Covered, in refrigerator.
■ Freeze: Not suitable.

CREAMY GARLIC CHEESE DIP

8oz package cream cheese
3 tablespoons sour cream
3 tablespoons whipping cream
2 cloves garlic, minced
2 tablespoons dry white wine
3 tablespoons chopped fresh parsley
3 tablespoons chopped fresh chives

Beat cheese in bowl with electric mixer until smooth. Add creams, garlic, wine and herbs, beat until combined; cover, refrigerate 1 hour. Serve with a variety of fresh vegetables.

Makes about 2 cups.

■ Dip can be made 2 days ahead.
■ Storage: Covered, in refrigerator.
■ Freeze: Not suitable.

SALAMI AND SUN-DRIED TOMATO WEDGES

8oz package soft cream cheese
3 tablespoons chopped fresh basil
6 sun-dried tomatoes, chopped
10 slices white bread
20 slices salami
10 pitted green olives, halved
10 pitted black olives, halved

Blend or process half the cheese with basil until smooth. Blend or process remaining cheese separately with tomatoes until smooth.

Cut rounds from bread the same size as the salami rounds. Spread a slice of salami with basil mixture, top with a bread round. Spread bread with tomato mixture, top with a slice of salami. Repeat with remaining salami, basil mixture, bread and tomato mixture, making 10 stacks. Cover, refrigerate 30 minutes.

Just before serving, cut stacks into 4 wedges, top each wedge with half an olive, secure with toothpick.

Makes 40.

■ Can be prepared 3 hours ahead.
■ Storage: Covered, in refrigerator.
■ Freeze: Not suitable.

BELOW: From left: Creamy Garlic Cheese Dip, Salami and Sun-Dried Tomato Wedges. RIGHT: Smoked Chicken Brioche.

SMOKED CHICKEN BRIOCHE

1 teaspoon active dry yeast
½ teaspoon superfine sugar
¼ cup warm water
2 cups all-purpose flour
1 tablespoon superfine sugar, extra
1 tablespoon chopped
    fresh oregano
2 eggs, lightly beaten
3oz (¾ stick) butter, softened
1 egg yolk
1 tablespoon milk
1 tablespoon rock salt

FILLING
2 tablespoons vegetable oil
1 small onion, chopped
½ cup sun-dried tomatoes,
    finely chopped
¼lb smoked chicken, finely chopped

Lightly grease mini muffin pans (4 teaspoon capacity). Combine yeast with sugar in bowl, stir in water, cover, stand about 10 minutes or until mixture is foamy.

Sift flour and extra sugar into bowl, stir in oregano, then combined eggs and yeast mixture, mix to a firm dough. Turn dough onto lightly floured surface, knead about 5 minutes or until smooth and elastic. Knead in small pieces of butter until all butter is incorporated; this should take about 5 minutes (mixture will be quite sticky at this stage).

Knead dough further 10 minutes or until smooth and elastic. Place dough in lightly oiled bowl, cover, stand in warm place about 1 hour or until doubled in size.

Knead dough until smooth, divide evenly into 32 portions. Remove a quarter of the dough from each portion. Flatten larger portions of dough into rounds, place a small amount of filling in center of each round, pinch dough up around filling so filling is enclosed. Place rounds pinched-side-down in prepared pans, brush tops of rounds lightly with a little of the combined egg yolk and milk.

Roll each remaining quarter of dough into a small ball, place on top of rounds in pans. Using a wooden skewer, push skewer through center of dough to base of pan, remove skewer. Brush tops with remaining milk mixture, sprinkle with salt. Stand in warm place about 15 minutes or until doubled in size.

Bake in 375°F oven 5 minutes, reduce heat to 350°F, bake further 10 minutes or until well browned and cooked through. Stand 2 minutes before cooling on wire racks. Repeat with remaining dough.

Filling: Heat oil in pan, add onion, cook, stirring, until onion is soft. Combine onion, tomatoes and chicken in bowl.

Makes 32.

■ Brioche can be made a day ahead.
■ Storage: Covered, in refrigerator.
■ Freeze: Cooked brioche suitable.
■ Microwave: Not suitable.

MINTED PEA AND WHOLE-WHEAT PASTRY BOATS

1¼ cups whole-wheat flour
3oz (¾ stick) butter
¼ cup sour cream
¼ cup sour cream, extra
fresh mint leaves

FILLING
1 cup (¼lb) frozen green
    peas, thawed
6 fresh mint leaves
pinch chili powder
1 green onion, chopped
¼ cup sour cream
1 egg

Sift flour into bowl, rub in butter. Stir in cream, mix to a firm dough. Knead dough gently on lightly floured surface until smooth; cover, refrigerate 30 minutes.

Roll pastry on lightly floured surface until 1/16 inch thick. Cut oval shapes to fit 3 inch long pastry boat tins, press pastry into tins, prick all over with fork. Place tins on baking sheet, bake in 400°F oven about 6 minutes or until dry to touch. Fill each pastry boat with 1½ level teaspoons of filling, bake further 8 minutes or until filling is set. Remove pastry boats from tins, cool on wire rack.

Just before serving, place extra sour cream in piping bag fitted with a small plain tube, pipe along centers of boats, top with mint leaves.
Filling: Blend or process all ingredients until smooth.

Makes about 40.

- Pastry boats can be made a day ahead. Filling can be made separately a day ahead.
- Storage: Pastry boats, in airtight container. Filling, covered, in refrigerator.
- Freeze: Unfilled pastry boats suitable.
- Microwave: Not suitable.

SARDINE CREAM ON PUMPERNICKEL

8oz package cream cheese
¼ cup whipping cream
2 tablespoons chopped fresh chives
2 tablespoons chopped fresh parsley
1 tablespoon chopped fresh dill
1 teaspoon lemon juice
1 teaspoon horseradish cream
dash Tabasco sauce
4oz can sardines, drained, mashed
½lb pumpernickel slices
2 tablespoons red lumpfish caviar
fresh dill sprigs

Beat cream cheese in small bowl with electric mixer until smooth. Add cream, herbs, juice, horseradish, Tabasco and sardines, beat until smooth. Cover, refrigerate 2 hours or until firm. Cut pumpernickel slices evenly into 2 inch x 1¼ inch rectangles.

Just before serving, spoon mixture into piping bag fitted with fluted tube, pipe onto pumpernickel, top with caviar and dill.

Makes about 40.

- Cream can be made a day ahead.
- Storage: Covered, in refrigerator.
- Freeze: Not suitable.

ABOVE: From left: Sardine Cream on Pumpernickel, Minted Pea and Whole-Wheat Pastry Boats.
RIGHT: From left: Duck and Orange Pate Crusties, Artichoke Cheese Berets, Tuna Cheese Creams.

ARTICHOKE CHEESE BERETS

3 x 13oz cans artichoke bottoms, drained
1 small red bell pepper
2oz packaged cream cheese
¼ teaspoon drained capers, finely chopped
1 dill pickle, finely chopped
2 teaspoons mayonnaise
1 hard-boiled egg, finely chopped

Cut a small slice from base of each artichoke; reserve slices. Cut half the pepper into small sticks; chop remaining pepper finely. Beat cheese in bowl until smooth. Stir in capers, dill pickle, mayonnaise, egg and chopped pepper. Fill artichokes with cheese mixture. Make a small cut in reserved artichoke slices, push in pepper sticks. Place slices on artichokes, beret style.

Makes about 24.

■ Recipe can be made 3 hours ahead.
■ Storage: Covered, in refrigerator.
■ Freeze: Not suitable.

TUNA CHEESE CREAMS

4oz package cream cheese
½ cup grated cheddar cheese
¼ cup grated fresh Parmesan cheese
1 tablespoon sour cream
14oz can tuna, drained
1 tablespoon chopped fresh chives
½ teaspoon seeded mustard
2 cups (5oz) sliced almonds, toasted

Blend or process cheeses, cream and tuna until smooth, stir in chives and mustard. Lightly crush almonds. Toss 2 level teaspoons of cheese mixture into nuts, press nuts on gently, shape into a ball. Repeat with remaining mixture and nuts; cover, refrigerate 1 hour before serving.

Makes about 55.

■ Recipe can be made a day ahead.
■ Storage: Covered, in refrigerator.
■ Freeze: Not suitable.

DUCK AND ORANGE PATE CRUSTIES

1 cup (2 sticks) unsalted butter
14oz duck and orange pate, chopped
1 teaspoon grated orange zest
1 tablespoon drained green peppercorns, crushed
⅓ cup chopped fresh chives
2 small French bread sticks

Beat butter in bowl with electric mixer until smooth. Gradually beat in pate, beat until smooth. Stir in zest, peppercorns and chives; mix well.

Cut each bread stick in half crossways. Using the end of a wooden spoon, scoop out bread to form a ½ inch shell. Spoon pate into piping bag fitted with plain tube, pipe mixture into centers of bread sticks. Wrap bread tightly in foil, refrigerate several hours or overnight.
Just before serving, cut bread sticks evenly into slices.

Makes about 55.

■ Rounds can be prepared a day ahead.
■ Storage: Covered, in refrigerator.
■ Freeze: Suitable.

FRESH BEET WITH SOUR CREAM IN ENDIVE LEAVES

You will need about 5 small Belgian endive for this recipe.

2 medium (7oz) uncooked beets, peeled, grated
3 tablespoons fresh orange juice
¼ cup vegetable oil
2 tablespoons chopped fresh chives
1 orange
⅓ cup sour cream
50 Belgian endive leaves
fresh chives, extra

Combine beets, juice, oil and chives in bowl. Thinly cut peel from orange, cut peel into fine strips. Add strips to pan of simmering water, simmer 5 minutes, drain.

Just before serving, spoon sour cream and beet mixture into endive leaves, top with peel and extra chives.

Makes 50.

- Beets and peel can be prepared 3 hours ahead.
- Storage: Covered, in refrigerator.
- Freeze: Not suitable.
- Microwave: Peel suitable.

SMOKED SALMON, CAPER AND DILL TRIANGLES

7oz packaged cream cheese
2 teaspoons lemon juice
1 tablespoon fresh dill sprigs
¼ teaspoon drained capers
12 slices white bread
6oz sliced smoked salmon

Blend or process cheese, juice, dill and capers until well combined. Spread 1 slice of bread with cheese mixture, top with a layer of salmon.

Spread a second slice of bread with cheese mixture, place cheese-side-down on salmon. Spread top with cheese mixture, top with a layer of salmon.

Spread a third slice of bread with cheese mixture, place cheese-side-down on salmon. Trim crusts from sandwich, cut into 8 triangles. Repeat with remaining bread, cheese mixture and salmon.

Makes 32.

- Triangles can be made 2 hours ahead.
- Storage: Covered, in refrigerator.
- Freeze: Not suitable

CURRIED CHICKEN AND TOMATO TARTLETS

25 slices white bread
2 tablespoons (¼ stick) butter, melted
1 tablespoon vegetable oil
fresh cilantro leaves

FILLING
2 tablespoons vegetable oil
1 onion, chopped
2 teaspoons curry powder
1 teaspoon apricot jam
3 tablespoons dry red wine
1 bay leaf
2 tablespoons water
½ cup mayonnaise
½ cup chopped cooked chicken
1 tomato, seeded, chopped
1 tablespoon chopped fresh cilantro

Lightly grease 12-hole tart trays. Cut 2 x 2 inch rounds from each slice of bread, roll rounds with rolling pin until thin. Place rounds into prepared trays, brush lightly with combined butter and oil. Place another tart tray on top of bread, press down, bake in 350°F oven for 8 minutes. Remove top tray, bake further 2 minutes or until bread cases are lightly browned; cool. Repeat with remaining bread rounds and butter and oil mixture.

Just before serving, spoon filling into bread cases, top with cilantro leaves.

Filling: Heat oil in pan, add onion and curry powder, cook, stirring, until onion is soft. Stir in jam, wine, bay leaf and water. Simmer, uncovered, about 10 minutes or until liquid is reduced by about three-quarters, strain, reserve the liquid; cool. Combine reserved liquid, mayonnaise, chicken, tomato and cilantro in bowl.

Makes 50.

- Cases can be made 2 days ahead. Filling can be made 3 hours ahead.
- Storage: Cases, in airtight container. Filling, covered, in refrigerator.
- Freeze: Not suitable.
- Microwave: Not suitable.

RIGHT: Clockwise from front: Fresh Beet with Sour Cream in Endive Leaves, Smoked Salmon, Caper and Dill Triangles, Curried Chicken and Tomato Tartlets.

AVOCADO PISTACHIO PATE WITH HERB TOASTS

1½ cups mashed avocado
4oz package cream cheese
2 green onions, chopped
1 small clove garlic, minced
1 teaspoon lemon juice
¼ teaspoon chili powder
3 tablespoons chopped
    pistachio nuts
1 teaspoon chopped fresh parsley

HERB TOASTS
2 Lebanese bread rounds
3 tablespoons butter, melted
½ teaspoon dried rosemary leaves
½ teaspoon dried basil leaves
½ teaspoon dried thyme leaves

Blend or process avocado, cheese, onions, garlic, juice and chili until smooth. Line 2 molds (1 cup capacity) with plastic wrap, sprinkle nuts into base of each mold, pour in avocado mixture. Cover, refrigerate 3 hours or until set.

Just before serving, unmold pate, remove plastic, sprinkle lightly with parsley. Serve pate with herb toasts.

Herb Toasts: Split bread rounds horizontally. Brush each half with butter; sprinkle with combined herbs. Place on baking sheets, bake in 350°F oven about 10 minutes or until lightly browned; cool. Break rounds into pieces.

Makes about 2 cups pate.

■ Both can be made a day ahead.
■ Storage: Herb toasts, in airtight container. Pate, covered, in refrigerator.
■ Freeze: Not suitable.
■ Microwave: Not suitable.

PIMIENTO, CORN AND BACON SPIRALS

4oz can creamed corn
2 tablespoons chopped fresh parsley
¾ cup fresh bread crumbs
6oz slices bacon, finely chopped
1 clove garlic, minced
5 green onions, chopped
7oz can pimientos, drained, chopped
⅓ cup grated fresh Parmesan cheese
8 sheets phyllo pastry
2 tablespoons (¼ stick) butter, melted
3 tablespoons vegetable oil

Combine corn, parsley and ¼ cup of the bread crumbs in bowl; mix well. Cook bacon in pan until crisp, add garlic and onions, cook, stirring, until onions are soft, drain on absorbent paper.

Combine bacon mixture with half the remaining bread crumbs in bowl. Combine pimientos, cheese and remaining bread crumbs in another bowl.

Layer 4 pastry sheets together, brushing each with some of the combined butter

and oil. Starting at a long edge and leaving 1¾ inch border along opposite edge, spread half the corn mixture lengthways over one-third of pastry. Cover center third with half the bacon mixture, sprinkle half the pimiento mixture over remaining third.

Tightly roll up pastry from the corn side, brush lightly with butter mixture. Place roll on tray, cover, refrigerate 1 hour.

Repeat with remaining pastry, butter

mixture, corn mixture, bacon mixture and pimiento mixture. Cut rolls into ½ inch slices, place slices on greased baking sheets, bake in 375°F oven about 15 minutes or until well browned. Cool spirals on trays.

Makes about 50.

■ Rolls can be made a day ahead.
■ Storage: Covered, in refrigerator.
■ Freeze: Uncooked rolls suitable.
■ Microwave: Not suitable.

FAR LEFT: Avocado Pistachio Pate with Herb Toasts.
ABOVE: Pimiento, Corn and Bacon Spirals.

MINI CHICKEN DRUMSTICKS

12 (about 2lb) chicken wings

MARINADE
**¼ teaspoon five-spice powder
¼ teaspoon turmeric
⅔ cup dry red wine
3 tablespoons vegetable oil
1 bay leaf
1 tablespoon barbeque sauce**

Cut first joint from wings. Separate second and third joints. Holding small end of third joint, trim around bone with sharp knife.

Cut, scrape and push meat down to large end. Using fingers, pull skin and meat over end of bone. Repeat with second joints, carefully removing 1 bone from each joint.

Combine drumsticks and marinade in bowl; mix well. Cover, refrigerate several hours or overnight.

Drain drumsticks, place on wire rack, place rack on baking sheet. Bake in 350°F oven about 10 minutes or until chicken is tender; cool. Wrap exposed ends of bone in foil, refrigerate until cold.

Marinade: Combine all ingredients in bowl; mix well.

Makes 24.

■ Drumsticks can be made a day ahead.
■ Storage: Covered, in refrigerator.
■ Freeze: Suitable.
■ Microwave: Suitable.

TOMATOES WITH CREAMY SMOKED OYSTER FILLING

**1lb cherry tomatoes
3½oz can smoked oysters, drained
3½oz packaged cream cheese
3 tablespoons lemon juice
fresh mustard cress**

Slice tops from tomatoes, scoop out seeds, drain tomatoes upside down on absorbent paper for 30 minutes. Blend or process oysters, cheese and juice; cover, refrigerate 30 minutes.

Spoon oyster mixture into piping bag fitted with fluted tube, pipe mixture into tomatoes, top with mustard cress.

Makes about 40.

■ Recipe can be made 3 hours ahead.
■ Storage: Covered, in refrigerator.
■ Freeze: Not suitable.

QUICK HERB TOASTIES

**3oz (¾ stick) butter
1 clove garlic, minced
3 tablespoons chopped fresh parsley
1 tablespoon chopped fresh basil
1 tablespoon chopped fresh chives
1 teaspoon chopped fresh thyme
10 slices white bread**

Beat butter, garlic and herbs in small bowl with electric mixer until creamy and combined. Cut crusts from bread, spread both sides of bread with herb butter, cut bread diagonally into quarters. Place quarters on ungreased baking sheet, bake in 350°F oven for about 20 minutes or until lightly toasted; cool.

Makes 40.

■ Toasties can be made a day ahead.
■ Storage: In airtight container.
■ Freeze: Uncooked toasties suitable.
■ Microwave: Not suitable.

RIGHT: Clockwise from front: Quick Herb Toasties, Mini Chicken Drumsticks, Tomatoes with Creamy Smoked Oyster Filling.

GRAVLAX ON MINI BUCKWHEAT BLINIS

It is correct that the salmon is not cooked in this recipe.

½lb fillet salmon
⅓ cup sugar
¼ cup coarse (Kosher) salt
2 teaspoons ground black pepper
⅓ cup chopped fresh dill
⅓ cup chopped fresh chives
3 tablespoons finely
   chopped avocado
2 teaspoons lemon juice
fresh dill sprigs, extra

BLINIS
¾ cup buckwheat flour
2 teaspoons sugar
1 egg, lightly beaten
½ cup milk
2 tablespoons (¼ stick) butter,
   melted
½ teaspoon cream of tartar
¼ teaspoon baking soda
1 tablespoon water

HERB BUTTER
¼ cup (½ stick) butter
1 teaspoon chopped fresh dill
1 teaspoon chopped fresh chives

Remove skin and bones from salmon. Combine sugar, salt, pepper and herbs in bowl. Sprinkle half the sugar mixture on tray covered with plastic wrap. Place salmon on top of sugar mixture, sprinkle remaining sugar mixture over top of salmon. Cover tightly with plastic wrap; refrigerate overnight.

Rinse salmon quickly and gently under cold water, pat dry with absorbent paper. Slice salmon thinly.

Just before serving, combine avocado and juice in bowl. Spread blinis evenly with herb butter, top with salmon slices, avocado and extra dill sprigs.

Blinis: Combine flour and sugar in bowl, gradually stir in combined egg, milk and butter, stir until smooth; cover, stand 1 hour. Stir in combined cream of tartar, soda and water.

Cook 4 blinis at a time. For each blini, spoon 2 level teaspoons of mixture into heated greased heavy-based pan, turn blinis when bubbles appear, cook until browned underneath. Cool on wire racks.

Herb Butter: Combine all ingredients in bowl; mix well.

Makes about 25.

■ Gravlax and herb butter can be made 2 days ahead. Blinis can be made 6 hours ahead.
■ Storage: Gravlax and herb butter, covered, in refrigerator. Blinis, in airtight container.
■ Freeze: Blinis suitable.
■ Microwave: Not suitable.

CHICKEN CHEESE BALLS

1 cup (5oz) chopped cooked chicken
4oz package cream cheese
1½ teaspoons French mustard
3 tablespoons lemon juice
1 cup (¼lb) salted mixed nuts

Blend or process chicken, cheese, mustard and juice until smooth; cover, refrigerate 1 hour.

Blend or process nuts until fine. Roll 2 level teaspoons of chicken mixture into a ball, toss in nuts.

Repeat with remaining mixture and nuts; cover, refrigerate for 1 hour.

Makes about 30.

■ Balls can be made a day ahead.
■ Storage: Covered, in refrigerator.
■ Freeze: Not suitable.

PUMPKIN SQUASH AND FETA ROUNDS

½lb pumpkin squash
1 medium (¼lb) potato
8 slices white bread
¼ cup ghee, melted
2oz feta cheese, chopped
2 teaspoons chopped fresh chives

HERB BUTTER
3 tablespoons butter
1 tablespoon chopped fresh chives
2 tablespoons chopped
   fresh parsley

Boil, steam or microwave squash and potato until tender, drain well. Mash squash and potato in bowl, push through sieve; cover, refrigerate until cold.

Cut 6 x 1½ inch rounds from each slice of bread. Combine ghee and bread rounds in bowl, stir until well coated, place rounds on baking sheet. Bake in 350°F for about 15 minutes or until rounds are lightly browned; cool.

Just before serving, thinly spread rounds with herb butter. Spoon squash mixture into piping bag fitted with fluted tube. Pipe mixture onto rounds, top with cheese and chives.

Herb Butter: Combine butter, chives and parsley in bowl; mix well.

Makes 48.

■ Rounds can be made a week ahead. Butter can be made 2 days ahead.
■ Storage: Rounds, in airtight container. Butter, covered, in refrigerator.
■ Freeze: Rounds and butter suitable.
■ Microwave: Vegetables suitable.

LEFT: Gravlax on Mini Buckwheat Blinis.
BELOW: From front: Pumpkin Squash and Feta Rounds, Chicken Cheese Balls.

CREAMY ASPARAGUS MOUSSE

14½oz can green asparagus spears
¼ cup (½ stick) butter
4 green onions, chopped
1 tablespoon all-purpose flour
½ cup heavy cream
2 teaspoons French mustard
dash Tabasco sauce
½ cup grated cheddar cheese
2 tablespoons gelatin
¼ cup water

Lightly oil 9 inch ring mold. Drain asparagus, reserve liquid. Blend or process asparagus until smooth. Heat butter in pan, add onions, cook, stirring, until soft. Stir in flour, cook until bubbling. Remove from heat, gradually stir in combined asparagus, reserved liquid, cream, mustard and sauce. Stir over heat until sauce boils and thickens.

Remove from heat, add cheese, stir until smooth, push mixture through sieve.

Sprinkle gelatin over water in cup, stand in small pan of simmering water, stir until dissolved; cool slightly.

Stir gelatin into asparagus mixture; pour into prepared mold; cover, refrigerate until set. Serve mousse with melba toast, if desired.

■ Mousse can be made a day ahead.
■ Storage: Covered, in refrigerator.
■ Freeze: Not suitable.
■ Microwave: Suitable.

QUAIL WITH PEPPERCORN AND PORT WINE SAUCE

12 quail breasts, skinned
2 tablespoons (¼ stick) butter
1 teaspoon vegetable oil

PEPPERCORN AND PORT SAUCE
2 green onions, chopped
¼ cup redcurrant jelly
2 teaspoons lemon juice
2 teaspoons port wine
1 teaspoon drained green
    peppercorns, crushed

Cut quail breasts in half. Heat butter and oil in pan, add quail, cook on both sides until lightly browned and tender, drain on absorbent paper; cool. Serve cold quail with peppercorn sauce.

Peppercorn and Port Wine Sauce: Drop onions into small pan of boiling water; remove from heat, stand 1 minute; drain. Combine onions, jelly, juice, port and peppercorns in pan, stir over heat until jelly is melted; cool to room temperature.

Makes 24.

■ Can be prepared 3 hours ahead.
■ Storage: Covered, in refrigerator.
■ Freeze: Uncooked quail suitable.
■ Microwave: Sauce suitable.

PARSLEY ANCHOVY DIP WITH CROUTONS

½ small onion, finely chopped
2 teaspoons drained capers, chopped
2 anchovy fillets, chopped
½ cup chopped fresh
    flat-leafed parsley
1 tablespoon lemon juice
¼ cup olive oil
6 pitted black olives, chopped

CROUTONS
2 small French bread sticks,
    thinly sliced
¼ cup (½ stick) butter, melted
2 tablespoons vegetable oil

Combine all ingredients in bowl; mix well, cover, refrigerate several hours. Serve dip with croutons.

Croutons: Brush bread with combined butter and oil, place on baking sheet, bake in 350°F oven about 5 minutes or until crisp; cool.

Makes about 1 cup dip.

■ Dip can be made a day ahead. Croutons can be made 2 days ahead.
■ Storage: Dip, covered, in refrigerator. Croutons, in airtight container.
■ Freeze: Croutons suitable.
■ Microwave: Not suitable.

ABOVE: From left: Quail with Peppercorn and Port Wine Sauce, Creamy Asparagus Mousse.
ABOVE RIGHT: From front: Parsley Anchovy Dip with Croutons, Red Bell Pepper Toasts.

RED BELL PEPPER TOASTS

2 large (1lb) red bell peppers
1 tablespoon olive oil
2 tablespoons dark brown sugar
⅓ cup dry white wine
3 tablespoons balsamic vinegar
3 tablespoons chopped fresh basil
⅓ loaf unsliced white bread
½ lime, thinly sliced

Cut peppers in quarters, remove membrane and seeds. Broil peppers, skin-side-up, until skin blackens and blisters; peel skin from peppers. Finely chop peppers. Heat oil in pan, stir in peppers and sugar, cook over low heat, covered, about 45 minutes or until peppers are soft, stirring occasionally. Stir wine and vinegar into pan, bring to boil, simmer, uncovered, about 15 minutes or until thick, remove from heat; strain, cool, stir in basil.

Cut bread into ¼ inch slices, cut 1 inch squares from slices, place squares on un-greased baking sheet. Bake in 350°F oven about 10 minutes or until lightly browned; cool. Spoon pepper mixture onto toast squares, top with lime wedges.

Makes about 80.
- Peppers can be prepared a day ahead; toasts made 2 days ahead.
- Storage: Peppers, covered, in refrigerator. Toast, in airtight container.
- Freeze: Toast squares suitable.
- Microwave: Not suitable.

BRANDIED CHEESES
ON PUMPERNICKEL

¼lb pepper cheese
¼lb neufchatel cheese
2 teaspoons brandy
pinch paprika
⅓ cup whipping cream
1 slice bacon, chopped
½lb pumpernickel slices
4 dried apricot halves, sliced
2 teaspoons chopped fresh chives

Blend or process cheeses, brandy and paprika until smooth. Transfer mixture to bowl. Whip cream in small bowl until soft peaks form, fold into cheese mixture; cover, refrigerate 30 minutes.

Cook bacon in pan until crisp, drain on absorbent paper; cool. Cut pumpernickel into ½ inch x 1½ inch fingers.
Just before serving, spoon cheese mixture into piping bag fitted with fluted tube. Pipe mixture onto pumpernickel, top with bacon, apricots and chives.

Makes about 48.

■ Cheese mixture can be prepared a
   day ahead.
■ Storage: Covered, in refrigerator.
■ Freeze: Not suitable.
■ Microwave: Bacon suitable.

PIQUANT FISH
AND LETTUCE PARCELS

We used mullet fillets in this recipe. It is correct that the fish is not cooked in this recipe, but appears and tastes cooked due to the marinating.

1lb fish fillets
¼ cup white vinegar
½ cup lemon juice
1 teaspoon salt
1 tablespoon chopped fresh dill
10 Boston lettuce leaves

Skin fillets, chop fish into ¾ inch cubes. Combine fish, vinegar, juice, salt and dill; cover, refrigerate several hours or overnight. Cut lettuce into ¾ inch strips.
Just before serving, drain fish, wrap in lettuce, secure with toothpicks.

Makes about 36.

■ Recipe can be prepared a day ahead.
■ Storage: Covered, in refrigerator.
■ Freeze: Not suitable.

CREAM CHEESE OLIVES
IN SALAMI

2oz packaged cream cheese
3 green onions, finely chopped
¼ teaspoon paprika
40 (¾lb) large pimiento-stuffed
   green olives
14oz sliced salami

Blend or process cheese, onions and paprika until smooth. Spoon mixture into piping bag fitted with small plain tube, pipe mixture into olives, pushing pimiento to end of each olive. Fold salami slices in half, secure around olive with toothpicks.

Makes 40.

■ Recipe can be made 3 hours ahead.
■ Storage: Covered, in refrigerator.
■ Freeze: Not suitable.

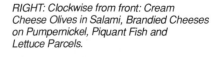

RIGHT: Clockwise from front: Cream Cheese Olives in Salami, Brandied Cheeses on Pumpernickel, Piquant Fish and Lettuce Parcels.

HERBED CHEESE AND SMOKED SALMON TARTLETS

1⅔ cups all-purpose flour
½ cup (1 stick) butter
2 eggs, lightly beaten
5oz smoked salmon slices
¼ cup fresh dill leaves

HERBED CHEESE
1lb neufchatel cheese
2 tablespoons lemon juice
2 tablespoons chopped fresh chives
3 tablespoons chopped fresh dill

Lightly grease 12-hole mini muffin pans (4 teaspoon capacity). Sift flour into bowl, rub in butter, add eggs, mix to a firm dough. Knead dough gently on lightly floured surface until smooth; cover, refrigerate 30 minutes.

Roll dough on floured surface until 1⁄16 inch thick. Cut 2¼ inch rounds from dough, place into prepared pans, prick all over with fork. Bake in 375°F oven about 10 minutes or until browned; cool in pans. Cut salmon into 2 inch strips.

Just before serving, fill pastry cases with herbed cheese, top with salmon strips and dill leaves.

Herbed Cheese: Beat cheese and juice in bowl with electric mixer until smooth. Stir in herbs; mix well.

Makes about 55.

- Pastry cases and herbed cheese can be prepared separately 2 days ahead.
- Storage: Pastry cases, in airtight container. Herbed cheese, covered, in refrigerator.
- Freeze: Unfilled pastry cases suitable.
- Microwave: Not suitable.

CURRIED YOGURT LAMB TARTLETS

1 sheet (10in x 10in) ready rolled
    shortcrust pastry
2 teaspoons chopped fresh mint

FILLING
7oz lamb fillet
1 tablespoon vegetable oil
¼ small red bell pepper,
    finely chopped
¼ cup plain yogurt
1 teaspoon curry powder
2 teaspoons chopped fresh mint

Cut 1¾ inch rounds from pastry, press into greased 1½ inch round fluted tart pans, place pans on baking sheet, bake in 350°F oven about 10 minutes or until

pastry is lightly browned; cool.
Just before serving, spoon filling into tartlet cases, sprinkle with mint.
Filling: Trim excess fat from lamb. Heat oil in pan, add lamb, cook until browned all over and tender; cool. Cut lamb into fine strips; combine with pepper, yogurt, curry powder and mint in bowl.

Makes about 25.

■ Tartlet cases can be made a week ahead; filling made a day ahead.
■ Storage: Tartlet cases in airtight container. Filling, covered, in refrigerator.
■ Freeze: Unfilled tartlet cases suitable.
■ Microwave: Not suitable.

BRANDIED BLUE CHEESE AND DATES ON CRACKERS

5oz mild blue vein cheese
3½oz packaged cream cheese
1 teaspoon brandy
1 teaspoon chopped fresh chives
4 fresh dates, pitted
25 water crackers
fresh parsley sprigs

Beat cheeses, brandy and chives in small bowl with electric mixer until combined. Cut dates into thin strips.
Just before serving, spoon cheese mixture into piping bag fitted with fluted tube, pipe onto crackers, top with date strips and parsley.

Makes about 25.

■ Cheese mixture can be prepared 2 days ahead.
■ Storage: Covered, in refrigerator.
■ Freeze: Not suitable.

LEFT: Herbed Cheese and Smoked Salmon Tartlets.
ABOVE: From left: Brandied Blue Cheese and Dates on Crackers, Curried Yogurt Lamb Tartlets.

LAMB ROLLS WITH ROSEMARY HOLLANDAISE

2 large (about 14oz) lamb fillets
2 tablespoons lemon juice
1 tablespoon vegetable oil
¼ teaspoon dried rosemary leaves
4 green onions

ROSEMARY HOLLANDAISE
1 tablespoon water
2 teaspoons lemon juice
¼ teaspoon dried rosemary leaves
6 black peppercorns
1 egg yolk
¼ cup (½ stick) butter, chopped

Trim excess fat from lamb. Combine juice, oil and rosemary in dish, add lamb, mix well; cover, refrigerate overnight.

Heat roasting pan, add lamb, cook over high heat until browned all over, bake in 350°F oven about 15 minutes or until tender; cool.

Cut green tops from onions, cut tops into thin strips. Cut lamb crossways into ¹⁄₁₆ inch slices (if lamb fillets are very thin, cut slices thicker and flatten with rolling pin). Spread each slice with rosemary hollandaise, roll up slices. Tie each roll with an onion strip.

Rosemary Hollandaise: Combine water, juice, rosemary and peppercorns in pan, bring to boil, simmer, uncovered, until liquid is reduced to 3 teaspoons, strain; reserve liquid. Whisk egg yolk and reserved liquid in top half of double saucepan or in heatproof bowl, whisk over simmering water until mixture begins to thicken. Remove from heat, whisk in butter gradually, whisk between additions.

Makes about 50.

■ Rolls can be made 6 hours ahead.
■ Storage: Covered, in refrigerator.
■ Freeze: Not suitable.
■ Microwave: Not suitable.

HERBED TOMATO LOBSTER

½ cup tomato juice
1 teaspoon chopped fresh chives
1 teaspoon chopped fresh basil
½lb uncooked lobster tail
1 tablespoon butter
1 teaspoon vegetable oil
1 tablespoon lime juice
5 slices white bread
2 tablespoons (¼ stick) butter, melted, extra

Combine tomato juice, chives and basil in bowl. Cut shell from underside of lobster. Remove flesh from shell, cut flesh into ¾ inch cubes.

Heat butter, oil and lime juice in pan, add lobster, cook, stirring, until just tender. Combine lobster with tomato mixture while hot; cover, refrigerate 3 hours.

Cut 4 x 1½ inch rounds from bread, brush both sides of rounds with extra butter. Place rounds on baking sheets, bake in 350°F oven 10 minutes, turn rounds, bake further 10 minutes or until browned.

Just before serving, drain lobster, serve on toast rounds.

Makes 20.
■ Lobster and toast rounds can be prepared separately a day ahead.
■ Storage: Lobster, covered, in refrigerator. Toast rounds, in airtight container.
■ Freeze: Not suitable.
■ Microwave: Not suitable.

PROSCIUTTO EGG ROLLS

12 quail eggs
¼ teaspoon grated lime zest
1½oz packaged cream cheese
2 tablespoons finely grated smoked cheese
1 teaspoon chopped fresh basil
6 slices (2oz) prosciutto

Place eggs in pan, cover with cold water, bring to boil, simmer, uncovered, for 3 minutes. Drain eggs; rinse under cold water; cool, remove shells.

Combine zest, cheeses and basil in bowl. Cut eggs in half. Cut prosciutto in half lengthways, cut into 2¾ inch strips. Spread cheese mixture onto each strip, wrap a prosciutto strip around egg.

Makes 24.
■ Recipe can be made 6 hours ahead.
■ Storage: Covered, in refrigerator.
■ Freeze: Filling suitable.
■ Microwave: Not suitable.

GINGER BEEF KABOBS

½ teaspoon wasabi
2 teaspoons light soy sauce
¼ cup mashed avocado
¼ teaspoon lemon juice
1 tablespoon butter, softened
¼ cup glace gingerroot
10 slices rare roast beef

Blend or process wasabi, sauce, avocado, juice and butter until smooth; cover, refrigerate 30 minutes.

Cut gingerroot into ½ inch pieces. Spread beef slices with avocado mixture, cut into ½ inch x 4¾ inch strips. Place a piece of gingerroot on center of each beef strip, fold strips in half, thread onto toothpicks. Cover, refrigerate 1 hour before serving.

Makes about 30.
■ Recipe can be made 3 hours ahead.
■ Storage: Covered, in refrigerator.
■ Freeze: Not suitable.

LEFT: From front: Lamb Rolls with Rosemary Hollandaise, Herbed Tomato Lobster, Prosciutto Egg Rolls.
BELOW: Ginger Beef Kabobs.

LAMB KABOBS WITH GARLIC MINT YOGURT

1lb ground lamb
1 onion, grated
1 teaspoon ground cumin
1 teaspoon ground coriander
3 tablespoons chopped fresh parsley
3 tablespoons vegetable oil

GARLIC MINT YOGURT
1 cup plain yogurt
3 tablespoons chopped fresh mint
1 clove garlic, minced

Process lamb, onion, cumin, coriander and parsley until smooth. Shape 2 level teaspoons of mixture into a ball. Repeat with remaining mixture. Thread balls onto skewers; cover, refrigerate several hours or overnight.

Heat oil in pan, add kabobs, cook until browned all over and cooked through; drain on absorbent paper. Cover, refrigerate several hours or until required. Serve kabobs with garlic mint yogurt.
Garlic Mint Yogurt: Combine all ingredients in bowl; mix well.

Makes about 25.

- ■ Recipe can be made a day ahead.
- ■ Storage: Covered, in refrigerator.
- ■ Freeze: Kabobs suitable.
- ■ Microwave: Not suitable.

CHICKEN TARRAGON PATE

1lb chicken livers
¼ cup port wine
½ cup (1 stick) butter
6 green onions, chopped
1 clove garlic, minced
1 tablespoon chopped fresh tarragon
½ cup whipping cream
2 tablespoons brandy
½ cup (1 stick) butter, extra

Combine livers and port in bowl; cover, refrigerate 2 hours.

Heat half the butter in pan, add onions and garlic, cook, stirring, until onions are soft. Add liver mixture, cook, stirring, until livers are lightly browned. Stir in tarragon, remove from heat.

Melt remaining butter in separate pan. Blend or process liver mixture until smooth. While motor is operating, gradually add butter, cream and brandy, process until smooth. Strain mixture into serving dishes; cover, refrigerate until firm.

Heat extra butter in pan until bubbling, stand 10 minutes; pour clear butter over pate. Cover, refrigerate until set. Serve pate with melba toast, if desired.

Makes about 2 cups.

- ■ Pate can be made 3 days ahead.
- ■ Storage: Covered, in refrigerator.
- ■ Freeze: Not suitable.
- ■ Microwave: Not suitable.

CHICKEN LIVER PATE

3 tablespoons butter
1 small onion, chopped
2 cloves garlic, chopped
½lb chicken livers
2 tablespoons port wine
1 teaspoon drained
    green peppercorns
2 tablespoons chopped fresh basil
¼ cup heavy cream
12 slices whole-wheat bread, toasted

Heat butter in pan, add onion and garlic, cook, stirring, until onion is soft. Add livers, cook, stirring, until livers change colour. Stir in port, peppercorns, basil and cream. Blend or process mixture until smooth, transfer to bowl; cover, refrigerate several hours or until firm.

Cut 4 x 1½ inch rounds from each slice of toast. Beat pate with electric mixer until smooth, spoon into piping bag fitted with fluted tube, pipe pate onto toasts, garnish with fresh herbs, if desired.

Makes 48.

- ■ Pate can be made 2 days ahead. Toasts can be made 6 hours ahead.
- ■ Storage: Pate, covered, in refrigerator. Toasts, in airtight container.
- ■ Freeze: Not suitable.
- ■ Microwave: Not suitable.

CAMEMBERT PASTRAMI SQUARES

1/4lb camembert
2 tablespoons (1/4 stick) butter
1 teaspoon mayonnaise
2 teaspoons chopped fresh chives
1/2lb pumpernickel squares
6 slices (3 1/2oz) pastrami
3 tablespoons chopped fresh
   chives, extra

Remove rind from camembert, stand camembert at room temperature until soft.

Beat butter, camembert and mayonnaise in small bowl with electric mixer until smooth, stir in chives. Spread each pumpernickel square with a level teaspoon of camembert mixture.

Cut pastrami into 3/4 inch squares, roll up, place onto squares, top with remaining cheese mixture and extra chives.

Makes about 20.

■ Recipe can be made 2 hours ahead.
■ Storage: Covered, in refrigerator.
■ Freeze: Not suitable.

SPINACH AND PIMIENTO CREPE ROLLETTES

3/4 cup all-purpose flour
3 eggs, lightly beaten
1 tablespoon vegetable oil
2/3 cup milk
10oz package frozen spinach, thawed

FILLING
2/3 cup sour cream
2 x 7oz cans pimientos,
   drained, chopped
3 tablespoons chopped fresh chives

Sift flour into bowl, gradually stir in eggs, oil and milk, beat until smooth. Squeeze excess moisture from spinach, stir spinach into batter.

Pour 3 to 4 tablespoons of batter into heated greased heavy-based crepe pan, cook until lightly browned underneath, turn crepe, cook until lightly browned underneath. Roll crepe while hot; cool. Repeat with remaining batter.

Unroll crepes, spread evenly with filling, roll up. Cut rolls into 3/4 inch slices; cover, refrigerate for 1 hour before serving.

Filling: Combine all ingredients in bowl. Makes about 55.

■ Recipe can be made a day ahead.
■ Storage: Covered, in refrigerator.
■ Freeze: Unfilled crepes suitable.
■ Microwave: Not suitable.

LEFT: From left: Lamb Kabobs with Garlic Mint Yogurt, Chicken Tarragon Pate.
ABOVE: Clockwise from top: Camembert Pastrami Squares, Chicken Liver Pate, Spinach and Pimiento Crepe Rollettes.

Roll pastry between sheets of baking paper until 1/8 inch thick. Cut 1 inch rounds from pastry, place onto lightly greased baking sheets, sprinkle half the rounds with paprika. Bake in 375°F oven about 8 minutes or until lightly browned; cool on sheets. Sandwich plain and paprika topped crisps with filling.

Filling: Stand cheese in bowl at room temperature 30 minutes. Beat in cream and basil, beat until smooth.

Makes about 45.

- ■ Crisps and filling can be made separately 2 days ahead.
- ■ Storage: Crisps, in airtight container. Filling, covered, in refrigerator.
- ■ Freeze: Unfilled crisps suitable.
- ■ Microwave: Not suitable.

MINI LETTUCE ROLLS WITH MINTY YOGURT SAUCE

1 iceberg lettuce
1 tablespoon butter
1 small red bell pepper, chopped
2 1/2oz button mushrooms, chopped
1 small zucchini, grated
1 small carrot, grated
2 green onions, chopped
3 tablespoons grated Parmesan cheese

MINTY YOGURT SAUCE
1 cup plain yogurt
3 tablespoons chopped fresh mint
1/2 teaspoon superfine sugar

Separate lettuce leaves, trim thick stalks from leaves. Drop leaves into pan of boiling water, drain immediately. Plunge into bowl of iced water, drain; pat dry with absorbent paper.

Heat butter in pan, add pepper, mushrooms, zucchini, carrot and onions, cook, stirring, until pepper is soft. Stir in cheese; cool to room temperature.

Cut lettuce leaves into 3 inch x 4 3/4 inch rectangles, top each rectangle with a rounded tablespoon of pepper mixture, fold in sides, roll up firmly. Serve rolls with sauce.

Minty Yogurt Sauce: Combine all ingredients in bowl.

Makes about 20.

- ■ Lettuce rolls can be made 1 hour ahead. Sauce, made a day ahead.
- ■ Storage: Covered, in refrigerator.
- ■ Freeze: Not suitable.
- ■ Microwave: Not suitable.

CILANTRO LAMB CROQUETTES

2 teaspoons grated fresh gingerroot
1lb ground lamb
2 cloves garlic, minced
1 onion, grated
1 tablespoon light soy sauce
3 tablespoons chopped fresh cilantro
1 medium carrot, grated
1 egg, lightly beaten
1 cup fresh bread crumbs
packaged unseasoned bread crumbs
oil for deep-frying

SAUCE
1/2 cup plum sauce
1/2 teaspoon light soy sauce
2 teaspoons chopped fresh cilantro

Press gingerroot between 2 spoons to extract juice; discard pulp. Combine juice, lamb, garlic, onion, sauce, cilantro, carrot, egg and fresh bread crumbs in bowl. Toss level tablespoons of mixture into packaged bread crumbs, shape into croquettes, place on baking sheet; cover, refrigerate 30 minutes. Deep-fry croquet-tes in hot oil until well browned and cooked through, drain on absorbent paper; cool. Cover, refrigerate until cold. Serve croquettes with sauce.
Sauce: Combine all ingredients in bowl.

Makes about 35.

- ■ Recipe can be made a day ahead.
- ■ Storage: Covered, in refrigerator.
- ■ Freeze: Uncooked croquettes suitable.
- ■ Microwave: Not suitable.

CHEESE CRISPS

1/2 cup self-rising flour
1/2 cup grated fresh Parmesan cheese
1/4 cup (1/2 stick) butter
2 teaspoons paprika

FILLING
1/2 cup grated havarti cheese
2 tablespoons heavy cream
2 teaspoons chopped fresh basil

Sift flour into bowl, stir in cheese. Rub in butter, press mixture firmly together into a ball (or process all ingredients to form a ball). Cover, refrigerate 30 minutes.

ABOVE LEFT: From back: Cilantro Lamb Croquettes, Cheese Crisps.
ABOVE RIGHT: Clockwise from left: Cheese and Bacon Dip with Caraway Crackers, Bocconcini and Prosciutto with Mustard Mayonnaise, Mini Lettuce Rolls with Minty Yogurt Sauce.

BOCCONCINI AND PROSCIUTTO WITH MUSTARD MAYONNAISE

3½oz prosciutto
7oz bocconcini, chopped

MUSTARD MAYONNAISE
½ cup mayonnaise
2 teaspoons seeded mustard
2 teaspoons chopped fresh basil

Cut prosciutto into ½ inch x 2¼ inch strips, wrap around bocconcini pieces, secure with toothpicks. Serve bites with mustard mayonnaise.
Mustard Mayonnaise: Combine mayonnaise, mustard and basil in bowl; mix well.

Makes about 35.

- Bites and mayonnaise can be made 6 hours ahead.
- Storage: Covered, in refrigerator.
- Freeze: Not suitable.

CHEESE AND BACON DIP WITH CARAWAY CRACKERS

4 slices bacon, thinly sliced
1lb ricotta cheese
⅓ cup sour cream
2 tablespoons chopped fresh chives
1 teaspoon seeded mustard
⅓ cup sliced almonds, toasted

CARAWAY CRACKERS
1lb small crackers
½ cup grated cheddar cheese
½ cup grated fresh Parmesan cheese
¼ teaspoon chili powder
1 teaspoon caraway seeds

Cook bacon in pan until crisp and well browned, drain on absorbent paper; cool.

Blend or process ricotta cheese and sour cream until smooth. Stir in bacon, chives, mustard and almonds. Serve dip with caraway crackers.

Caraway Crackers: Place crackers on baking sheets in single layer, sprinkle evenly with combined cheeses, chili and seeds. Bake in 350°F oven about 10 minutes or until cheese is melted; cool.

Makes about 2 cups dip.

- Dip and crackers can be made several hours ahead.
- Storage: Dip, covered, in refrigerator. Crackers, in airtight container.
- Freeze: Not suitable.
- Microwave: Not suitable.

109

SMOKED TURKEY QUICHES

4 sheets phyllo pastry
¼ cup (½ stick) butter, melted
3 tablespoons cranberry sauce
4 slices (about 2½oz) smoked turkey
    breast roll, sliced
¼ cup grated cheddar cheese
⅓ cup milk
⅓ cup heavy cream
1 egg, lightly beaten
2 tablespoons chopped fresh chives

Lightly grease mini muffin pans (4 teaspoon capacity). Layer pastry sheets together, brushing each sheet lightly with butter. Cut 2¼ inch rounds from pastry, ease into prepared pans. Bake in 350°F oven about 5 minutes or until lightly browned. If pastry cases are puffed, flatten centers slightly while warm; cool.

Divide cranberry sauce, turkey and cheese between cases. Combine remaining ingredients in jug, pour into cases. Bake in 350°F oven about 15 minutes or until set; cool.

Makes about 30.

◼ Pastry cases can be made 2 days ahead. Quiches can be cooked 2 hours ahead.
◼ Storage: Covered, in refrigerator.
◼ Freeze: Not suitable.
◼ Microwave: Not suitable.

BUTTON MUSHROOMS WITH CREAMY EGG

30 (about 10oz) button mushrooms
3 hard-boiled eggs
1 tablespoon sour cream
2 tablespoons mayonnaise
2 teaspoons chopped fresh chives
2 tablespoons chopped fresh parsley
¼ teaspoon ground black pepper
¼ teaspoon French mustard

Remove stems from mushrooms; keep stems for another use. Mash eggs with remaining ingredients in bowl.
Just before serving, spoon egg mixture into mushrooms.
Makes 30.

◼ Egg filling can be made a day ahead. Mushrooms, filled 1 hour ahead.
◼ Storage: Covered, in refrigerator.
◼ Freeze: Not suitable.

SESAME BEEF ON CUCUMBER

1lb piece rump steak
¼ cup dark soy sauce
1 clove garlic, minced
1 tablespoon sesame seeds
1 teaspoon Oriental sesame oil
1 tablespoon vegetable oil
1 long green cucumber
¼ small red bell pepper

Trim excess fat from steak, wrap steak in plastic wrap, freeze 30 minutes.

Cut steak into very thin slices, cut slices into thin strips. Combine strips, sauce, garlic, seeds and sesame oil in shallow glass dish; cover, refrigerate 3 hours.

Heat half the oil in pan, add half the beef, cook for about 2 minutes or until well browned all over; drain, cool. Repeat with remaining oil and beef.

Peel 4 thin strips lengthways from cucumber skin, cut cucumber crossways into ¼ inch slices. Cut pepper into long thin strips. Top cucumber slices with beef and pepper.

Makes about 30.

◼ Recipe can be made 3 hours ahead.
◼ Storage: Covered, in refrigerator.
◼ Freeze: Not suitable.
◼ Microwave: Not suitable.

BELOW: From left: Smoked Turkey Quiches, Button Mushrooms with Creamy Egg.
RIGHT: Clockwise from front: Sesame Beef on Cucumber, Smoked Eel Pate, Turkey Lettuce Parcels.

TURKEY LETTUCE PARCELS

3½oz roast turkey breast roll, chopped
1 tablespoon mango
   chutney, chopped
3 tablespoons mayonnaise
1 teaspoon seeded mustard
20 red leaf lettuce leaves

Combine turkey, chutney, mayonnaise and mustard in bowl. Remove thick centers from lettuce leaves. Drop leaves into pan of boiling water, drain immediately, drop into bowl of iced water. Drain leaves, pat dry with absorbent paper.

Place a level teaspoon of turkey mixture on center of a lettuce leaf, fold up to form a parcel. Repeat with remaining lettuce and turkey mixture.

Makes 20.

■ Filling can be made a day ahead. Parcels can be made an hour ahead.
■ Storage: Covered, in refrigerator.
■ Freeze: Not suitable.
■ Microwave: Not suitable.

SMOKED EEL PATE

14oz smoked eel, skinned, boned
½ cup sour cream
1 tablespoon lemon juice
1 tablespoon marsala
3 tablespoons butter, melted

Blend or process eel, cream, juice and marsala until smooth. Push mixture through sieve to remove fine bones. Stir in butter; cover, refrigerate until firm. Serve with selection of fresh salad vegetables and melba toast, if desired.

Makes about 1 cup.

■ Pate can be made 2 days ahead.
■ Storage: Covered, in refrigerator.
■ Freeze: Suitable.

MARINATED MUSHROOMS

⅔ cup cider vinegar
½ cup vegetable oil
1 teaspoon sugar
3 tablespoons chopped fresh parsley
1 clove garlic, minced
¾lb (about 35) button
mushrooms, halved

Combine vinegar, oil, sugar, parsley and garlic in bowl; mix well. Add mushrooms, stir to coat; cover, refrigerate several hours or overnight. Drain mushrooms before serving.

Makes about 70.

■ Can be made 2 days ahead.
■ Storage: Covered, in refrigerator.
■ Freeze: Not suitable.

SMOKED EEL AND DILL PICKLE SQUARES

3 tablespoons mayonnaise
2 teaspoons chopped fresh dill
2 teaspoons chopped fresh cilantro
3oz packaged mini toast
5oz smoked eel, skinned, sliced
2 dill pickles, sliced
1 teaspoon chopped fresh red
chili pepper

Combine mayonnaise, dill and cilantro in bowl; spread thinly over toasts. Arrange eel and dill pickles over mayonnaise, sprinkle with a little chili.

Makes about 30.

■ Squares can be made 2 hours ahead.
■ Storage: Covered, in refrigerator.
■ Freeze: Not suitable.

APRICOT CHICKEN BALLS

¾lb ground chicken
½ cup packaged, unseasoned
bread crumbs
1 egg
½ cup finely chopped dried apricots
½ cup finely chopped macadamias
1 tablespoon light soy sauce
1 tablespoon chopped fresh cilantro
fresh cilantro leaves, extra

Blend or process chicken, bread crumbs, egg, apricots, nuts, sauce and chopped cilantro until well combined. Roll 2 level teaspoons of mixture into a ball, top with an extra cilantro leaf. Repeat with remaining mixture and extra cilantro. Place balls in top half of steamer in single layer, cook, covered, over boiling water for about 8 minutes or until cooked through; cool, refrigerate.

Makes about 50.

■ Balls can be made a day ahead.
■ Storage: Covered, in refrigerator.
■ Freeze: Uncooked balls suitable.
■ Microwave: Not suitable.

RIGHT: Clockwise from back: Apricot Chicken Balls, Smoked Eel and Dill Pickle Squares, Marinated Mushrooms.

BEEF WALDORF TARTS

**1 sheet (10in x 10in) ready rolled
    shortcrust pastry**
**3 tablespoons chopped red
    bell pepper**

FILLING
3½oz sliced rare roast beef, chopped
¼ cup finely chopped apple
½ teaspoon lemon juice
3 tablespoons finely chopped celery
**2 tablespoons finely chopped
    walnuts or pecans**
1 tablespoon chopped dill pickle
3 tablespoons sour cream
2 teaspoons mayonnaise

Lightly grease 12-hole tart trays. Cut 1¾
inch rounds from pastry, ease pastry into
prepared trays, cover with rounds of
baking paper, fill with dried beans or rice.
Bake in 350°F oven about 7 minutes,
remove paper and beans, bake further 5
minutes or until lightly browned; cool.

Just before serving, spoon filling into
pastry cases, top with pepper.
Filling: Combine beef, apple, juice,
celery, nuts, dill pickle, cream and mayonnaise in bowl; mix well.

Makes about 25.

- Pastry cases can be made 2 days
  ahead. Filling, made 2 hours ahead.
- Storage: Pastry cases, in airtight con-
  tainer. Filling, covered in refrigerator.
- Freeze: Unfilled pastry cases suitable.
- Microwave: Not suitable.

CHICKEN AND PRUNE PINWHEELS

⅔ cup (5oz) pitted prunes
**4 large boneless, skinless chicken
    breast halves**
4 cups water
2 large chicken bouillon cubes, crumbled

Soak prunes in boiling water for about
15 minutes or until softened. Drain

prunes, blend or process until smooth.
Pound chicken between sheets of baking
paper until thin. Spread chicken with
prune mixture, roll up chicken from narrow ends, wrap rolls tightly in foil.

Combine water and bouillon cubes in
pan, bring to boil, add rolls to water. Simmer, covered, about 15 minutes or until
chicken is cooked. Drain rolls; cool,
refrigerate until cold.
Just before serving, unwrap rolls, cut
into ½ inch slices.

Makes about 20.

- Can be made 2 days ahead.
- Storage: Covered, in refrigerator.
- Freeze: Uncooked rolls suitable.
- Microwave: Not suitable.

SALMON AND SPINACH PINWHEELS

8 spinach leaves, roughly chopped
1 egg
½ cup canned drained flaked
   salmon
2 green onions
¼ cup all-purpose flour
½ cup milk
2½oz packaged cream
   cheese, softened
2 tablespoons red lumpfish caviar

Steam spinach until tender, drain, squeeze excess moisture from spinach. Blend or process spinach, egg, salmon and onions until combined. With motor operating, gradually add flour and milk, process until smooth.

Pour 3 to 4 tablespoons of batter into heated greased heavy-based crepe pan; cook until lightly browned underneath. Turn crepe, brown on other side. Repeat with remaining batter; cool. Spread crepes with a thin layer of cream cheese, then caviar. Roll crepes tightly; cover, refrigerate for 1 hour.

Just before serving, cut crepe rolls into ½ inch slices.

Makes about 30.

■ Pinwheels can be made a day ahead.
■ Storage: Covered, in refrigerator.
■ Freeze: Not suitable.
■ Microwave: Not suitable.

NUTTY CHICKEN RIBBON SANDWICHES

15 slices grain bread
3oz (¾ stick) butter, softened
1½ cups (7oz) finely chopped
   cooked chicken
1 stalk celery, finely chopped
2 tablespoons sour cream
3 tablespoons mayonnaise
⅓ cup chopped pistachios

Spread 1 side of each bread slice with butter. Combine chicken, celery, sour cream, mayonnaise and nuts in bowl; mix well. Spread 5 slices of bread with half the chicken mixture, top with buttered bread, buttered-side-down. Spread with remaining chicken mixture, top with buttered bread, buttered-side-down.

Cut crusts from sandwiches, cut sandwiches into thirds, cut each third into 2 pieces.

Makes 30.

■ Can be made 3 hours ahead.
■ Storage: Covered, in refrigerator.
■ Freeze: Suitable.

LEFT: From left: Beef Waldorf Tarts, Chicken and Prune Pinwheels.
BELOW: From front: Nutty Chicken Ribbon Sandwiches, Salmon and Spinach Pinwheels.

CORN AND PIMIENTO FRITTERS WITH HERBED TUNA

4oz can whole-kernel corn, drained
⅓ cup chopped drained pimientos
3 eggs, lightly beaten
1 teaspoon lemon pepper
⅔ cup all-purpose flour
fresh thyme sprigs

TOPPING
2 (about 10oz) tuna steaks
¼ teaspoon dried chili flakes
2 teaspoons chopped fresh cilantro
2 teaspoons chopped fresh basil
1 teaspoon chopped fresh thyme
1 teaspoon grated lime zest
1 tablespoon lime juice
1 tablespoon vegetable oil
¼ teaspoon sugar

HERB CREAM
½ cup sour cream
1 teaspoon chopped fresh basil
1 teaspoon chopped fresh chives
½ teaspoon chopped fresh thyme
1 teaspoon lime juice

Combine corn, pimientos, eggs and pepper in bowl, stir in sifted flour, mix well. Using 2 level teaspoons of mixture per fritter, spoon mixture into hot greased pan, cook until lightly browned underneath. Turn fritters, brown other side; drain on absorbent paper, cool.

Just before serving, top fritters with topping, herb cream and thyme sprigs.

Topping: Place tuna in bowl, combine remaining ingredients in separate bowl, pour over tuna; cover, refrigerate 1 hour. Add undrained tuna mixture to heated pan, cook for about 5 minutes each side or until cooked through; cool. Cut tuna into thin slices.

Herb Cream: Combine sour cream, herbs and juice in bowl.

Makes about 30.

- Fritters and topping can be made a day ahead. Herb cream can be made 3 days ahead.
- Storage: Covered, in refrigerator.
- Freeze: Not suitable.
- Microwave: Not suitable.

WHOLE-WHEAT PIKELETS WITH CREAMY EGG TOPPING

1 cup whole-wheat flour
2 teaspoons double-acting baking powder
1 egg, lightly beaten
1 cup milk
2 teaspoons seeded mustard
1 tablespoon butter, melted
1oz salmon roe

TOPPING
4 hard-boiled eggs, halved
3 tablespoons mayonnaise
3 tablespoons sour cream
3 tablespoons chopped fresh chives

Sift flour into bowl, gradually stir in combined egg and milk; beat to a smooth batter. Stir in mustard and butter.

Drop teaspoons of mixture into heated greased heavy-based pan. Turn pikelets when bubbles appear, brown on other side; cool.

Just before serving, spread topping onto pikelets, top with roe. Sprinkle with extra chives, if desired.

Topping: Remove yolks from eggs, mash yolks in bowl. Finely chop egg whites, stir into yolks with mayonnaise, sour cream and chives; mix well.

Makes about 90.

- Can be prepared 6 hours ahead.
- Storage: Pikelets, in airtight container. Topping, covered, in refrigerator.
- Freeze: Pikelets suitable.
- Microwave: Not suitable.

LEFT: Corn and Pimiento Fritters with Herbed Tuna.
ABOVE: Clockwise from back: Pimiento Prosciutto Eggs, Sun-Dried Tomatoes with Cabanossi and Cheese, Whole-Wheat Pikelets with Creamy Egg Topping.

PIMIENTO PROSCIUTTO EGGS

6 hard-boiled eggs, halved
2 tablespoons mayonnaise
1 tablespoon whipping cream
1 tablespoon chopped drained canned pimiento
2 tablespoons chopped fresh basil
3 slices (about 1oz) prosciutto, finely chopped
1 tablespoon chopped fresh basil, extra
1 tablespoon chopped drained canned pimiento, extra

Remove yolks from eggs, mash yolks in bowl with mayonnaise and cream. Stir in pimiento, basil and prosciutto. Spoon mixture into egg whites, top with extra basil and extra pimiento.

Makes 12.

- Eggs can be made 3 hours ahead.
- Storage: Covered, in refrigerator.
- Freeze: Not suitable.

SUN-DRIED TOMATOES WITH CABANOSSI AND CHEESE

12in piece cabanossi
14 sun-dried tomato halves, drained
7oz matured provolone cheese, chopped
⅓ cup fresh basil leaves

Slice cabanossi diagonally into ¼ inch slices. Cut each tomato half into thirds. Thread cabanossi, tomato, cheese and basil onto cocktail skewers.

Makes 42.

- Kabobs can be made 3 hours ahead.
- Storage: Covered, in refrigerator.
- Freeze: Not suitable.

117

BRIE, EGG AND SMOKED TROUT TRIANGLES

2 eggs, lightly beaten
3 tablespoons butter, softened
2 teaspoons grated lime zest
6 slices white bread
3½oz sliced smoked trout
¼lb brie
6 slices rye bread
¼ cup sour cream

Pour half the egg into heated greased 8 inch omelet pan, cook until just set. Remove omelet from pan, cool. Repeat with remaining egg.

Beat butter and zest in bowl until combined. Spread white bread slices with butter mixture, top with trout. Remove rind from brie, beat brie in bowl until smooth, spread evenly over trout. Cut omelets to fit bread, place on brie. Spread rye bread with cream, place, cream-side-down, onto omelet layer; press lightly.

Cut crusts from sandwiches. Cut sandwiches into 8 triangles.

Makes 48.

■ Can be made 4 hours ahead.
■ Storage: Covered, in refrigerator.
■ Freeze: Not suitable.

ABOVE: Brie, Egg and Smoked Trout Triangles.
ABOVE RIGHT: Clockwise from back: Bacon Crackers with Parsely Dip, Olives in Cheese Pastry, Mini Minted Lamb Pikelets.

BACON CRACKERS WITH PARSLEY DIP

½lb slices bacon, chopped
⅔ cup self-rising flour
¼ cup whole-wheat flour
½ cup grated fresh Parmesan cheese
¼ cup cornmeal
½ teaspoon caraway seeds
3 tablespoons butter
⅓ cup plain yogurt
3 tablespoons French mustard

PARSLEY DIP
1 cup chopped fresh parsley
¼ cup chopped fresh mint
1 clove garlic, minced
1 small red bell pepper, finely chopped
1 small onion, finely chopped
¼ cup olive oil
3 tablespoons lemon juice
½ teaspoon ground black pepper

Cook bacon in pan until crisp; drain on absorbent paper; cool. Blend or process bacon, flours, cheese, cornmeal and seeds until bacon is finely chopped. Add butter, process until well combined; transfer mixture to bowl. Stir in combined yogurt and mustard, mix to a soft dough. Knead dough on lightly floured surface until smooth; cover, refrigerate dough 30 minutes.

Roll dough on lightly floured surface until ¹⁄₁₆ inch thick. Cut into 2¼ inch rounds, place rounds onto lightly greased baking sheets. Bake in 350°F oven about 15 minutes or until browned; cool.

Parsley Dip: Combine all ingredients in bowl; cover, refrigerate for 4 hours.

Makes about 50 crackers.

Makes about 1½ cups dip.

■ Crackers can be made a week ahead. Dip can be made a day ahead.
■ Storage: Crackers, in airtight container. Dip, covered, refrigerated.
■ Freeze: Not suitable.
■ Microwave: Not suitable.

MINI MINTED LAMB PIKELETS

⅓ cup self-rising flour
2 tablespoons whole-wheat flour
¼ teaspoon baking soda
1 egg, lightly beaten
⅓ cup milk
½ teaspoon white vinegar
2 teaspoons butter, melted
2 teaspoons chopped fresh mint

MINT BUTTER
¼ cup (½ stick) butter, softened
3 tablespoons mint jelly

MINTED LAMB
1 tablespoon butter
1 clove garlic, minced
7oz lamb fillets
1 tablespoon mint jelly

Sift dry ingredients into bowl, gradually stir in combined egg, milk and vinegar, beat to a smooth batter; stir in butter (or blend or process these ingredients until smooth).

Drop level teaspoons of batter into heated greased heavy-based pan. Cook until bubbles appear, turn pikelets, brown other side; cool.

Just before serving, spread mint butter over pikelets, top with minted lamb, sprinkle with mint.

Mint Butter: Beat butter and jelly in bowl until combined.

Minted Lamb: Heat butter and garlic in pan, add lamb, cook until well browned all over and tender; cool. Cut lamb into thin strips, return to pan with jelly, stir over heat until combined; cool.

Makes about 40.

■ Recipe can be prepared a day ahead.
■ Storage: Pikelets, in airtight container. Mint butter and minted lamb, covered, in refrigerator.
■ Freeze: Pikelets suitable.
■ Microwave: Not suitable.

OLIVES IN CHEESE PASTRY

1 cup all-purpose flour
pinch cayenne pepper
3½oz butter
1¼ cups (5oz) grated
    cheddar cheese
50 small pimiento stuffed green olives
1 egg, lightly beaten
poppy seeds

Process flour, pepper and butter until combined. Add cheese, process until mixture forms a ball. Knead dough on lightly floured surface until smooth; cover, refrigerate 30 minutes. Drain olives on absorbent paper.

Roll pastry between sheets of baking paper until ¹⁄₁₆ inch thick. Cut 1¾ inch rounds from pastry, top each round with an olive, fold pastry around olives to enclose, roll into balls.

Dip tops of balls in egg, then seeds. Place balls onto greased baking sheet; cover, refrigerate 30 minutes.

Bake in 375°F oven about 15 minutes or until browned; cool.

Makes 50.

■ Recipe can be made a day ahead.
■ Storage: In airtight container.
■ Freeze: Not suitable.
■ Microwave: Not suitable.

LEMON GRASS AND CHILI BEEF PARCELS

2 teaspoons butter
14oz beef tenderloin, chopped
3 tablespoons finely chopped fresh
    lemon grass
2 small fresh red chili peppers,
    finely chopped
4 green onions, chopped
3 tablespoons tomato paste
¼ cup water
12 large cabbage leaves

Heat butter in pan, add beef, cook, stirring, until well browned. Stir in lemon grass, chilies and onions, cook, stirring, until onions are soft. Stir in paste and water; cool to room temperature.

Trim thick stalks from cabbage leaves; cut leaves in half. Steam leaves until wilted, drain on absorbent paper. Spoon beef mixture onto narrow end of each leaf half, fold sides in, roll up, secure with toothpicks. Cover, refrigerate until cold.

Makes 24.

■ Parcels can be made 6 hours ahead.
■ Storage: Covered, in refrigerator.
■ Freeze: Not suitable.
■ Microwave: Cabbage suitable.

LAMB IN CUCUMBER CUPS

4 green cucumbers
1 tablespoon vegetable oil
6 green onions, finely chopped
½ stalk celery, finely chopped
1 small fresh green chili pepper,
    finely chopped
1lb ground lamb
1 small clove garlic, minced
½ teaspoon grated fresh gingerroot
1 tablespoon dark soy sauce
½ teaspoon honey
2 teaspoons cornstarch
1 tablespoon water
2 tablespoons chopped fresh cilantro

Cut cucumbers into ½ inch slices. Carefully scoop out some seeds from each slice to form a cup. Heat oil in pan, add onions, celery and chili, cook, stirring, until celery is soft.

Add lamb, garlic and gingerroot, cook, stirring, until lamb is browned. Stir in blended sauce, honey, cornstarch and water, stir until mixture boils and thickens slightly; cool. Spoon lamb mixture into cucumber cups, sprinkle with cilantro.

Makes about 50.

■ Cups can be made 6 hours ahead.
■ Storage: Covered, in refrigerator.
■ Freeze: Not suitable.
■ Microwave: Not suitable.

CHICKEN AND BEET PHYLLO NESTS

3 sheets phyllo pastry
2 tablespoons (¼ stick) butter, melted
1 cup (5oz) finely chopped
    cooked chicken
¼ cup sour cream
½ teaspoon garam masala
fresh cilantro leaves

BEET RELISH
1 small (¼lb) uncooked beet
1 small onion, finely chopped
1 tablespoon superfine sugar
¼ teaspoon grated lemon zest
1 teaspoon lemon juice
¼ cup white vinegar
¼ teaspoon coriander seeds
¼ teaspoon cuminseed
1 clove garlic, minced
pinch chili powder

Lightly grease mini muffin pans (4 teaspoon capacity). Layer pastry sheets together, brushing each sheet lightly with butter; cut into 2½ inch squares. Gently press squares into prepared pans. Bake in 375°F oven about 5 minutes or until well browned. Cool in pan 5 minutes before turning onto wire rack to cool.

Combine chicken, cream and garam masala in bowl. Spoon a level teaspoon of mixture into each pastry case.

Just before serving, spoon beet relish into nests, top with cilantro leaves.

Beet Relish: Cut beet into ¹⁄₁₆ inch slices, cut into ¾ inch strips. Combine beet, onion, sugar, zest, juice, vinegar, seeds, garlic and chili in pan. Bring to boil, simmer, uncovered, about 20 minutes or until most of the liquid is evaporated.

Makes about 30.

■ Pastry cases can be made a day
    ahead. Relish can be made
    2 weeks ahead.
■ Storage: Pastry cases, in airtight
    container. Relish, covered, in
    refrigerator.
■ Freeze: Not suitable.
■ Microwave: Relish suitable.

ABOVE: Chicken and Beet Phyllo Nests.
RIGHT: Clockwise from back: Crab Mousse, Lamb in Cucumber Cups, Lemon Grass and Chili Beef Parcels.

CRAB MOUSSE

2 (about 1lb) cooked crabs
1 small red bell pepper
½ cup sour cream
3 tablespoons lemon juice
2 tablespoon chopped fresh chives
2 teaspoons gelatin
1 tablespoon water

Lightly oil 2 molds (¾ cup capacity). Remove flesh from body and claws of crab; you will need 6oz crab meat.

Cut pepper into quarters, remove seeds and membrane, broil pepper skin-side-up on oven tray until skin blackens and blisters; cool. Remove skin from pepper, chop pepper roughly.

Blend or process pepper, sour cream, juice and chives until smooth. Sprinkle gelatin over water in cup, stand in small pan of simmering water, stir until gelatin is dissolved; cool. Fold crab and gelatin into pepper mixture, pour into prepared molds; cover, refrigerate until set.

Just before serving, unmold mousse onto plates, serve with crackers.

Makes about 1½ cups.

■ Mousse can be made a day ahead.
■ Storage: Covered, in refrigerator.
■ Freeze: Not suitable.
■ Microwave: Gelatin suitable.

Glossary

Here are some terms, names and alternatives to help everyone understand and use our recipes perfectly.

ALCOHOL: is optional but adds special flavor; use juice or water to make up the liquid content in a recipe.

ALMONDS, SLICED: almonds cut into thin slices.

BACON SLICES: we used thick slices where specified.

BAKING PAPER: non-stick parchment paper used for lining cake pans and baking sheets.

BAMBOO SKEWERS: can be used instead of metal skewers if soaked in water overnight or for several hours to prevent burning during cooking. They are available in several different lengths.

BARBEQUE SAUCE: a spicy sauce available from most supermarkets.

BOK CHOY (Chinese chard)**:** discard stems, use leaves and young tender parts of stems. It requires only a short cooking time such as stir-frying.

BOUILLON CUBES: available in beef, chicken or vegetable. Use 1 large crumbled bouillon cube to every 2 cups water. Remember that these cubes contain salt so be sure to allow for this when seasoning food.

BREAD CRUMBS:
FRESH: use 1- or 2-day-old bread; crumbed by grating, blending or processing.
UNSEASONED PACKAGED: use fine packaged unseasoned bread crumbs.

BUTTER: use salted or unsalted (sweet) butter.

BUTTERMILK: is now made by adding a culture to skim milk to give a slightly acid flavor; skim milk can be substituted, if preferred.

CABANOSSI: a type of sausage; also known as cabana.

CARDAMOM: an expensive spice with an exotic fragrance. It can be bought in pod, seed or ground form.

CHEESE:
BOCCONCINI: small balls of mild, delicate cheese packaged in water or whey to keep them white and soft. The water should be just milky and cheese should be white; yellowing indicates that it is too old.
CHEDDAR: use a full-flavored, firm cheddar.
CREAM CHEESE: unripened, smooth, spreadable cheese.
FETA: a fresh, soft Greek cheese with a slightly crumbly texture and a sharp, salty flavor.
GRUYERE: a Swiss cheese with small holes and a nutty, slightly salty flavor.
HAVARTI: a semi-soft Danish cheese.
JARLSBERG: a Norwegian cheese made from cows' milk; it has large holes and a mild nutty taste.
NEUFCHATEL: soft, unripened or fresh curd cheese. It resembles cream cheese but contains more moisture.
PARMESAN: sharp-tasting cheese used as a flavor accent.
PEPPER: a semi-soft cheese containing green peppercorns.
PEPPERED CAMEMBERT: a fresh camembert cheese containing green peppercorns with herbs in the rind.
PROCESSED CHEDDAR: we used a processed cheese which has 22 percent fat content.
PROVOLONE: we used an aged provolone with a firm grainy texture and pronounced spicy flavor.
RICOTTA: we used cheese with 10 percent fat content.
SOFT CREAM CHEESE: also known as Light Cream Cheese, do not substitute for cream cheese in our recipes.
SWISS: we used a mild-flavored Swiss style cheese.

CHESTNUTS: we used canned whole chestnuts (marrons).

CHICKEN:
CHICKEN LOAF: processed pressed luncheon style loaf.
PREMIUM: we used a large sliced chicken loaf available at delicatessens.

CHICORY: curly-leafed vegetable mainly used in salads.

CHILIES: are available in many different types and sizes. The small ones (bird's eye or bird peppers) are the hottest. Use tight rubber gloves when chopping fresh chilies as they can burn your skin.

CHILI POWDER: ground dried chilies.

CHIPOLATA SAUSAGES: small cocktail sausages in various flavors.

COCONUT CREAM: available in cans and cartons in supermarkets and Asian stores; canned coconut milk can be substituted, although it is not as thick.

CILANTRO: also known as Chinese parsley and coriander, is essential to many South-East Asian cuisines. A strongly flavored herb, use it sparingly until you are accustomed to the unique flavor. Parsley can be used instead but tastes quite different. The leaves, stems and roots can be used.

CORN, CREAMED: available in various sized cans from most supermarkets.

CRAB, BLUE SWIMMER: any fresh crab can be substituted.

CRANBERRY SAUCE: cranberries preserved in sugar syrup; has an astringent flavor.

CREAM:
HALF-AND-HALF: thin pouring cream.
HEAVY: use when specified in recipes.
WHIPPING: is specified when necessary in recipes.
SOUR: a thick commercially cultured soured cream.

CRUNCHY OAT BRAN CEREAL: a low-fat, high-fibre toasted breakfast cereal based on oat bran.

CRUSHED NUTS: crushed peanuts.

CUCUMBER: we used large green cucumbers (telegraph cucumbers) and small green cucumbers (Lebanese cucumbers) in this book.

CUMIN: available in seed or ground form; it is another component of commercial curry powder.

DILL PICKLE: pickled baby cucumber.

DOUBLE-ACTING BAKING POWDER: a raising agent consisting of an alkali and an acid. It is mostly made from cream of tartar and baking soda in the proportion of 1 level teaspoon of cream of tartar to ½ level teaspoon baking soda. This is equivalent to 2 level teaspoons double-acting baking powder.

EGG NOODLES: we used fine fresh egg noodles in this book. They are available from Asian food stores.
EGG PASTRY SHEETS: we used 4 inch squares in packages available from Asian food stores.

FENNEL SEEDS: fennel seeds are a component of curry powder.
FISH FILLETS, WHITE: we used firm, white fish fillets.
FISH SAUCE: an essential ingredient in the cooking of a number of South-East Asian countries, including Thailand and Vietnam. It is made from the liquid drained from salted, fermented anchovies. It has a very strong aroma and taste. Use sparingly until you acquire the taste.
FIVE-SPICE POWDER: a pungent mixture of spices which includes cinnamon, cloves, fennel, star anise and Szechuan peppers.
FLOUR:
BESAN: is made from ground chick peas (garbanzo beans); also known as gram or chick pea flour.
BUCKWHEAT: flour milled from buckwheat.
WHITE SELF-RISING: substitute all-purpose flour and double-acting baking powder in the proportion of 1 cup plain flour to 2 level teaspoons of baking powder. Sift together several times before using.
WHOLE-WHEAT: whole-wheat flour without the addition of baking powder.
FRENCH BREAD STICK: long, thin, crisp white bread stick.

GARAM MASALA: there are many variations of the combinations of cardamom, cinnamon, cloves, coriander, cumin and nutmeg used to make up this spice used often in Indian cooking. Sometimes pepper is used to make a hot variation. It is readily available in jars.
GHEE: clarified butter.
GINGERROOT:
FRESH OR GREEN: scrape away skin and grate, chop or slice gingerroot as required. Fresh, peeled gingerroot can be preserved with enough dry sherry to cover; keep in jar in refrigerator; it will keep for months.
GLACE: fresh gingerroot preserved in sugar syrup; crystallised gingerroot can be substituted; rinse off the sugar with warm water, dry gingerroot well before using.
GROUND: should not be substituted for fresh gingerroot in any recipe.
PICKLED: is dyed and preserved in rice wine and sugar; we used the pink variety.
GRAND MARNIER: an orange-flavored liqueur. Cointreau can be substituted.

GREEN GINGER WINE: an Australian-made alcoholic sweet wine infused with fresh gingerroot.

HERBS: we have specified when to use fresh or dried herbs. We used dried (not ground) herbs in the proportion of 1:4 for fresh herbs, eg, 1 teaspoon dried herbs instead of 4 teaspoons chopped fresh herbs.
HOISIN SAUCE: a thick sweet Chinese barbeque sauce made from salted black beans, onions and garlic.
HORSERADISH CREAM: paste of horseradish, oil, mustard and flavorings.

JAM: conserve.

LAMB:
FILLET: a very small tender cut found between the loin and chump.
RIBLETS: rib ends closest to the breast, also called spareribs.
LARD: fat obtained from melting down and clarifying pork fat; it is available packaged.
LEMON GRASS: available from Asian food stores and needs to be bruised or chopped before using. It will keep in a jug of water at room temperature for several weeks; the water must be changed daily. It can be bought dried; to reconstitute, place several pieces of dried lemon grass in a bowl; cover with hot water, stand 20 minutes; drain. This amount is a substitute for 1 stem of fresh lemon grass.
LEMON PEPPER SEASONING: is a blend of crushed black pepper, salt, lemon, herbs and spices.
LEMON SPREAD: lemon curd or lemon cheese.
LETTUCE: we used iceberg lettuce unless otherwise stated.
LOBSTER: crayfish.
LUMPFISH CAVIAR: this is not a true caviar, but an economical substitute; red and black varieties are available.

MARSALA: a sweet fortified wine.
MILK: we used full cream milk.
MINT JELLY: contains sugar, food acids, pectin, mint etc.
MIRIN: a sweet rice wine used in Japanese cooking. Substitute 1 teaspoon sugar and 1 teaspoon dry sherry for each 4 teaspoons mirin.
MULLET: an oily, strong-flavored variety of deep sea fish.
MUSTARD:
DRY: in powdered form.
SEEDED: a French style of mustard with crushed mustard seeds.

OIL: polyunsaturated vegetable oil.
OLIVE: virgin oil is obtained only from the pulp of high-grade fruit. Pure olive oil is pressed from the pulp and kernels of second grade olives.
ORIENTAL SESAME OIL: made from roasted, crushed white sesame seeds. Use in small quantities. Do not use for frying.

ONIONS, GREEN: also known as spring onions and scallions.
OYSTER CASES: small vol-au-vent cases made from puff or flaky pastry, available in 2oz and 2½oz packages.
OYSTER-FLAVORED SAUCE: a rich brown sauce made from oysters cooked in salt and soy sauce, then thickened with starches.

PARSLEY (flat-leafed): also known as Italian or continental parsley.
PASTRAMI: highly seasoned smoked beef ready to eat when bought.
PEPITAS: pumpkin seed kernels.
PIMIENTOS: red bell peppers (capsicums) canned or bottled in brine or vinegar; sometimes called sweet red pimientos or sweet red peppers.
PLUM SAUCE: a dipping sauce which consists of plums preserved in vinegar, sweetened with sugar and flavored with chilies and spices.
PORK, BARBEQUED: roasted pork fillets available from many Asian fresh food and specialty stores.
POTATOES: we used old potatoes unless otherwise specified.
SWEET: we used the orange-colored variety unless otherwise specified.

PROSCIUTTO: uncooked, unsmoked ham cured in salt; it is ready to eat when purchased.
PRUNES: dried plums.
PUFF PASTRY: available frozen from supermarkets in blocks and ready-rolled sheets.

RICE PAPER: edible paper available from Asian food stores and gourmet food shops.

SALMON: we used a farmed variety of fish available all year.
SAMBAL OELEK (uelek or ulek): a paste made from ground chilies and salt.
SEAFOOD STICKS: made from Alaskan pollack flavored with crab.
SHRIMP: most of the recipes in this book use uncooked (green) shrimp; they must be shelled and deveined before use.

SOYA CRISPS: savory snacks made from an extruded soy bean mixture.

SOY SAUCE: made from fermented soy beans. The light sauce is generally used with white meat for flavor, and the darker variety with red meat for color. There is a multi-purpose salt-reduced sauce available, also Japanese soy sauce. It is personal taste which sauce you use.

SPINACH: a soft-leaved vegetable, more delicate in taste than Swiss chard; however, young Swiss chard can be substituted.

SQUID (calamari): a type of mollusc. Cleaned squid hoods are available.

SUGAR:

BROWN: we used dark or light as specified.

CONFECTIONERS': powdered sugar.

SUPERFINE: fine granulated table sugar.

SWISS CHARD: remove coarse white stems, cook green leafy parts as individual recipes indicate.

TABASCO SAUCE: made with vinegar, hot red chili peppers and salt. Use sparingly.

TACO SAUCE: found in supermarkets among Mexican ingredients.

TERIYAKI SAUCE: based on the lighter Japanese soy sauce; contains sugar, spices and vinegar.

TOMATO:

KETCHUP: we used tomato ketchup.

PUREE: canned, pureed tomatoes (not tomato paste). Use fresh, peeled, pureed tomatoes, if preferred.

TOMATO SUPREME: a canned product consisting of tomatoes, onions, celery, bell peppers and seasonings.

TOMATOES, SUN-DRIED: are dried tomatoes sometimes bottled in oil.

TURMERIC: a member of the gingerroot family, its root is ground and dried, giving the rich yellow powder which gives curry its characteristic color; it is not hot in flavor; use in small quantities.

VINEGAR: we used both white and brown (malt) vinegar in this book.

BALSAMIC: originated in the province of Modena, Italy. Regional wine is specially processed then aged in antique wooden casks to give pungent flavor.

WASABI: powdered green horseradish used in Japanese cooking. Substitute hot mustard powder or fresh, grated horseradish. It is usually sold in cans and mixed to a paste with cold water.

WATER CHESTNUTS: small white crisp bulbs with a brown skin. Canned water chestnuts are peeled and will keep for about 1 month, covered, in refrigerator.

WATER CRACKERS: savory crackers.

WONTON SKINS: are thin squares or rounds of fresh noodle dough. Cover with a damp cloth to prevent drying out while using.

WORCESTERSHIRE SAUCE: is a spicy sauce used mainly on red meat.

YEAST: ¼oz package active dry yeast (2 level teaspoons) is equal to ½oz fresh compressed yeast.

ZEST: colored skin of citrus fruit.

CUP & SPOON MEASURES

To ensure accuracy in your recipes use standard measuring equipment.

a) 8 fluid oz cup for measuring liquids.

b) a graduated set of four cups – measuring 1 cup, half, third and quarter cup – for items such as flour, sugar, etc.
When measuring in these fractional cups level off at the brim.

c) a graduated set of five spoons: tablespoon (½ fluid oz liquid capacity), teaspoon, half, quarter and eighth teaspoons.
All spoon measurements are level.

We have used large eggs with an average weight of 2oz each in all our recipes.

Index

Home Library
Salads
Sensational recipes for all occasions

Home Library
COUNTRY
COOKING

Home Library
Healthy Heart
Cookbook

Home Library
VEGETARIAN
COOKING

THE BEST **Home Library**
SEAFOOD
RECIPES

Home Library
Italian
COOKING CLASS COOKBOOK

Home Library
CHICKEN
COOKBOOK
PLUS duck, quail, turkey, goose and more

Home Library
PASTA
COOKBOOK
More than 170 recipes

Home Library
CHINESE
COOKING CLASS COOKBOOK

Home Library
STARTERS AND SOUPS

Home Library
BEGINNERS'
COOKBOOK

Home Library
FINGER FOOD
Best ever party food
Tempting hot and cold savouries
Dips, spreads and finishing dips